Too Easy to Keep

Life-Sentenced Prisoners and the
Future of Mass Incarceration

STEVE HERBERT

UNIVERSITY OF CALIFORNIA PRESS

University of California Press, one of the most distin-
guished university presses in the United States, enriches
lives around the world by advancing scholarship in the
humanities, social sciences, and natural sciences. Its
activities are supported by the UC Press Foundation and
by philanthropic contributions from individuals and
institutions. For more information, visit www.ucpress.edu.

University of California Press
Oakland, California

Library of Congress Cataloging-in-Publication Data

Names: Herbert, Steven Kelly, 1959– author.
Title: Too easy to keep : life-sentenced prisoners and the
    future of mass incarceration / Steve Herbert.
Description: Oakland, California : University of
    California Press, [2019] | Includes bibliographical
    references and index. |
Identifiers: LCCN 2018023684 (print) | LCCN 2018025473
    (ebook) | ISBN 9780520971875 (e-book) | ISBN
    9780520300507 (cloth : alk. paper) | ISBN 9780520300514
    (pbk. : alk. paper)
Subjects: LCSH: Prisoners—Social aspects—United
    States.
Classification: LCC HV9469 (ebook) | LCC HV9469 .H47 2018
    (print) | DDC 365/.60973—dc23
LC record available at https://lccn.loc.gov/2018023684

Manufactured in the United States of America

27   26   25   24   23   22   21   20   19
10   9   8   7   6   5   4   3   2   1

Contents

Preface and Acknowledgments

My first extensive interactions with incarcerated men occurred in 2013, in a small fluorescent-lit classroom in the Washington State Reformatory. I was there to meet with the prisoner advisory council for a nonprofit organization, University Beyond Bars, which provides college-preparatory and college-level instruction for those incarcerated at the reformatory.

I was planning a "mixed enrollment" course, one that would include roughly equal numbers of students from University Beyond Bars and from the Department of Law, Societies, and Justice at the University of Washington. The course would be taught entirely inside the reformatory. I was at the prison to discuss both the class and a miniseminar that I planned to offer first so I could become familiar with teaching inside.

It was a pleasant conversation. Each man from the prisoner advisory council greeted me warmly with a firm handshake as he entered the room. I was offered a cup of pomegranate tea. Although one prisoner's questions betrayed some suspicion about my motivations, there was a pervasive enthusiasm about my plans. I left the meeting feeling optimistic.

That feeling only intensified throughout the course of the miniseminar. For four class sessions, the participants engaged in thoughtful and probing conversations about some recent and controversial U.S. Supreme Court rulings. These were classes like thousands of others I have taught over my career. They were special only because of the location.

Much the same could be said about the subsequent mixed-enrollment course. Despite some initial awkwardness, the class quickly fell into a nice rhythm. Small group discussions demonstrated significant energy, and large group debates birthed telling insights and creative analysis. It was as good a classroom dynamic as any I had ever seen.

I must admit that I was surprised by this outcome. As I write this now, some years later, my surprise shames me.

My surprise was born out of ignorance, out of my own implicit stereotypes of prisoners. Despite my understanding of the dynamics behind mass incarceration, I was still taken aback that so many prisoners possessed the engaged intellects they so readily displayed. I should have known better; I should have known that our prisons house many, many thoughtful and capable people.

I was also surprised to learn that many of those stellar University Beyond Bars students were serving extremely long sentences, up to and including life without the possibility of parole. This reality shamed me even more. I was more than a little troubled that the state in which I lived—and for which I worked—would condemn perfectly mature and valuable individuals to life behind bars with no hope of release.

My surprise and shame motivated this book. I seek here to shed light on a reality about which most U.S. citizens are unaware. It is a little-known fact that life-sentenced prisoners are a large and growing component of America's incarcerated population. Despite increased awareness that the United States leads the world in its rate of incarceration, less attention falls on the rise of life sentences. This neglect is troublesome. Unless the trend is reversed, thousands of individuals who deserve release will be condemned to die in prison. This morally questionable outcome is compounded further by cost considerations. Aging prisoners, unsurprisingly, are expensive to house. As these prisoners pile up inside America's institutions, states like Washington will face staggering price tags.

Such moral and fiscal challenges should be addressed directly and transparently in considered public conversations. My hope is that this book can help stimulate such conversations by documenting many of the consequences of the increase in life sentences.

* * *

While researching and writing this volume, I incurred many debts. I cannot hope to repay those debts, but I must at least acknowledge them.

I first thank the Washington Department of Corrections for granting me the necessary access to acquire the interview data upon which my analysis principally rests. Staff at the Monroe Correctional Complex worked assiduously to schedule the extensive number of interviews, and many of them sat for interviews themselves. Their assistance with this project was invaluable.

The good people at University Beyond Bars enabled my first efforts at prison education. I especially thank Stacey Reeh, who was unfailingly responsive, considerate, and bureaucratically adept. Without her, the mixed-enrollment effort would never have launched, and this book would never have resulted.

That the mixed-enrollment courses continue is due significantly to Tim and Connie Wettack. Their generosity and their example are inspirations. Tim and Connie also provided my introduction to the Concerned Lifers Organization, whose efforts at prison reform energize me and countless others.

At the University of Washington, I am blessed to be part of the supportive community that is the Department of Law, Societies, and Justice. There are too many members of that community to individually thank here, but the faculty, students, and staff all motivate me each and every day. Their collective enthusiasm for prison-based education, and for thoughtful attention to punishment policy, has done much to keep me going. It is simply an honor to work alongside them.

For her support of the Department of Law, Societies, and Justice and of our efforts to institutionalize prison-based education, I thank Judy Howard. Her enthusiasm was unwavering and consequential.

I received much-appreciated financial support from the Royalty Research Fund at the University of Washington. Much of this book was conceived, written, and edited at the Whiteley Center. I thank the staff there, and especially Kathy Cowell, for making it such a welcoming and contemplative place.

Useful feedback on earlier versions of this manuscript came from Katherine Beckett, Reed Klein, Hannah Schwendeman, and two anonymous reviewers. I thank them for that, just as I thank Maura Roessner at University of California Press, who displayed welcome early interest and then valuable patience while I labored more slowly than I expected. Bonita Hurd's copyediting was outstanding and much appreciated.

In addition to her comments on the manuscript, Katherine Beckett influenced this work in ways too numerous and notable to measure. Her own dedication to criminal justice reform is beyond remarkable. I draw inspiration from her example more than she likely knows, and appreciate it more than I can adequately express.

AnnaRose and Jesse have engaged in more conversations about prisons than perhaps they wanted, but I hope I have helped spark their own political commitments. It is certainly a privilege to watch their personal concerns for justice unfold, and an unmatchable gift to be present in their lives.

Finally, and most importantly, I must thank the twenty-one lifers who agreed to talk with me. They willingly answered my many and probing questions with a striking degree of honesty, and bravely allowed themselves to become emotionally vulnerable in my presence. I can only hope that I have returned their generosity with an analysis that is sensitive and telling, and which draws beneficent attention to their plight.

The Easy Keeper

"Easy keeper."

It is a phrase often used inside prisons that house life-sentenced inmates, a term of art deployed commonly by prisoners and prison staff alike. It describes a prisoner, usually one sentenced to life, who practices a steady daily routine and who provides little to no disruption. Here's one prison staff member describing this group: "Some guys don't break any rules. You know, they're the easy keepers. They do their jobs, they go to school, they don't commit any infractions, they keep their cells clean and tidy, and they follow the rules. And usually those are our LWOPs.[1] They follow the rules. They're usually our easiest keepers." Here's another staff member, a high-ranking officer in the custody staff: "If they've been in for even ten years, but ten to twenty, twenty-five years, we call them easy keepers, because you don't have to do anything. They know the routine, they know what they're doing, they've been there, done that. They probably learned by now that they don't want any trouble—you know, they get their perks and their privileges. They're set in their thing, so they just do their job, very polite, no issues." Or, as one member of the custody staff explained, "Life withouts, they're easy to maintain."

Beyond being easy to maintain, life-sentenced prisoners commonly exert a stabilizing influence on the prisons in which they live. Indeed, prison staff frequently express a desire for more such prisoners. Said one staff member, when asked whether lifers were good for the institution where he worked,

> They are. If we could have more life-without-paroles here, it would calm the facility down. The people that are making this place disruptive are the young kids that come in that might only have to do six to nine months, or twelve months. They come in, they disrupt the facility, then they leave. The elderly guys, this is their home; they're not going anywhere. They're life-without-parole; they want everything to run smoothly. They like routine. They don't like it when the routine is messed up.

Even more, both staff and prisoners claim that when trouble is brewing, everyone looks to lifers to provide calm. Here's how Kevin,[2] a life-sentenced prisoner, describes that dynamic: "Well, [lifers] keep the peace. When things start building, lifers will work with these youngsters and say, 'Let's find a better solution. Let's do something different.' And a lot of times, it works."

It might seem as if those with life sentences would find continuing reasons to rebel. With little to no hope of release, they might well give up and express their frustration in myriad and perhaps disruptive ways. However, Leonard, another prisoner, made plain that lifers do have much to lose if they are not careful:

> LEONARD: A lifer, even though it seems like, on paper, he doesn't have anything to lose, he's got the most to lose because of what he's trying to achieve in the facility that he's in. He's trying to do the right thing, make the right choices, stay with family,

EFVs,[3] programming. All these things which would be ruined immediately if he were to act out. They're the most stable. They're the best card to play. The staff here know that. They know that most of the lifers don't get into any trouble at all. Very seldom.

HERBERT: And do they stabilize the rest of the institution?

LEONARD: Absolutely. There's a lot of men here that keep things calmer than what they normally would be if they just stood out, stayed away from the problems.

Another prisoner, Oscar, made essentially the same point: "What I always consider the more typical, main population lifer is a very stable personality who wants to get through each day one at a time, move on through with the least amount of acid on the water, and go through whatever else; and they tend to be stabilizers."[4]

For Isaac, a prisoner, it is not at all hard to spot an easy keeper:

They just have a certain aura about them. When they're in the chow hall, they're usually pretty polite. They don't run around talking about other people. They have a set program, and you see what they're doing by their actions. You see they're not getting in trouble, they're not yelling at the cops, being disrespectful, yelling at ten o'clock nighttime, calling people crazy names—they're not saying all that. You can just tell a lifer—a guy who's done time—and a guy who hasn't. I think the biggest thing is the respect factor of it. It's very noticeable.

As I describe in greater detail in the next chapter, the stabilization provided by the life-sentenced population stems significantly from their efforts to provide mentorship and guidance to younger prisoners. They do this, in part, because of their desire to have a calm and quiet environment. But they also commonly possess a felt need to perform some measure of atonement for their past transgressions. Regardless of motivation, however, both prisoners and prison staff indicate that the easy-keeper population is a consistently positive force.

TOO EASY TO KEEP?

In this book I focus on these "easy keepers." I try to convey the role that well-stabilized life-sentenced prisoners play in the institutions that house them. I explore how they came to adopt this role and why they play it. I also seek to understand what enables and impedes their quests for a meaningful life.

Importantly, I also examine why prison staff might both welcome and fear the presence of an increased number of life-sentenced prisoners. On the one hand, staff appreciate the calming influence easy keepers exert; prisoners who are well-adapted to life inside make the institution more manageable. On the other hand, life-sentenced prisoners will necessarily age, decline, and die, and these natural processes pose challenges for prison staff. As a prisoner ages, his mobility will decrease, his physical health decline, his cognitive abilities deteriorate. Each of these changes creates complications for any institution, but especially a prison, where security and strict routine are paramount concerns.

This book's title, *Too Easy to Keep,* has a double meaning. Each of these meanings nods to one of my main arguments. First, far too many of those with life sentences should not remain in prison. Many have demonstrated through their daily lives that they are reasonably well-adjusted, capable of assuming responsibility for their lives, and willing to be of consistent service to others. That they have become easy keepers suggests that their personal transformation is so significant that they deserve consideration for release. They are too "easy" to deserve being kept any longer.

The second meaning focuses on the political dynamics that confine too many people to prison. Various sentencing policies, and the heartless politics that drive them, have generated a large and expanding population of life-sentenced prisoners in the United States. This happened too easily and occurred with little consideration of the downstream implications of the increasing numbers of aging prisoners. Even if many lifers are easy keepers today, their eventual declines will tax prison systems considerably. Those prisoners are left largely to their own devices to find purpose in their lives, and prison staff are forced to continually improvise to meet the pressing demands of an aging population. This book describes many of the unavoidable challenges our prisons face as lifers steadily accumulate. If we acknowledge such challenges, it becomes harder to justify sentences that condemn so many individuals to a death in prison. Our politics, in other words, have made it far too easy to keep prisoners who deserve release. These politics need reconsideration.

A FOCUS ON EASY KEEPERS

Life-sentenced prisoners in the United States are now too numerous to escape considered public attention. In 2016, there were 206,268 prisoners serving what amounts to a life sentence.[5] This means that about one in seven prisoners in the United States in 2016 was serving life.[6] Put differently, nearly one in three of the world's life-sentenced population is confined in the United States.

The number of those with a life sentence has more than quadrupled since 1984,[7] a reality that, unsurprisingly, is generating a larger population of aging prisoners. Projections suggest that as many as one-third of American prisoners will be fifty-five or older by 2030. That would represent an increase in this population of 4,400 percent from 1980 to 2030.[8]

Given the rampant racial disparities in the American criminal justice system, it is not surprising that nearly half of the U.S. lifer population is African American.[9] In some states, particularly those in the Deep South, two-thirds or more of lifers are African American. Latinx prisoners compose another 15 percent of the lifer population nationally. In other words, fully two-thirds of life-sentenced prisoners in the United States are people of color.[10]

The sizeable number of American lifers is a fairly new phenomenon. Even as late as the 1970s, a life sentence rarely meant exactly that.[11] Life-without-parole laws became popular in that decade, however, driven in part by the temporary suspension of capital punishment.[12] Today, forty-nine states and the federal government all have LWOP as a sentencing option.[13] This punishment is often meted out for aggravated murder and other violent crimes, but it can also be imposed on so-called habitual offenders, commonly through "three strikes and you're out" laws.[14] These policy shifts were part and parcel of a more massive "race to incarcerate" that infected American politics in a particularly virulent form beginning in the late 1970s and lasting into the 1990s.[15] These politics led to policies that increased the likelihood of the imposition of a life sentence; they also made it less likely that parole-eligible prisoners would be granted release.[16] Besides LWOP sentences, the general proliferation of longer sentences has increased the number of "virtual," or "de facto," life sentences. These result when a prisoner's expected release date postdates his or her expected life span.[17]

The increase in life-sentenced prisoners continues to occur despite two countervailing trends. The first is that rates of crime—and this notably includes rates of violent crime—have been on a steady decline during the same time period.[18] The rise of life sentences is thus not a response to any surge in serious crime. A second countervailing trend is the slow reduction in the overall rate of incarceration in the United States, largely owing to reduced penalties for less-serious crimes, such as those connected to drug use and distribution.[19] Yet any significant reductions in incarceration are notably constrained by the increase in life sentences. Unless the number of lifers is reduced, it will be difficult to effect a meaningful overall reduction in prison populations across the United States.[20]

This tremendous growth in lifers foretells a wide range of consequences, both for the prisoners who receive life sentences and the institutions that must house them. I seek, in what follows, to outline many of these consequences. My focus is less on the fiscal consequences—although these are considerable—and more on the human dimensions of this radical set of incarceration policies. To chart these dynamics, my study is necessarily qualitative.

THE DATA AND THE SETTING

I rely primarily on interview data to substantiate my arguments. The interviews I conducted fell into two categories.

The first consists of interviews with life-sentenced prisoners.[21] In the summer and fall of 2015, I interviewed twenty-one such prisoners in two medium-security prisons in Washington State.[22] Each prisoner was interviewed two or three times in sessions that averaged seventy-five minutes. The interview schedule was structured chronologically. Each prisoner discussed his time in prison from entry to the present. The interviews were semi-structured, and thus each prisoner had considerable allowance to discuss various issues of concern to him. I sought to understand how prisoners adjusted to their life sentences, what challenges they faced, what changes to prison life they desired, and how they envisioned their futures.

Of those I interviewed, thirteen were white, five African American, two Latinx, and one American Indian. The racial composition of my interview sample thereby largely mirrored the racial composition of the broader lifer population in the state of Washington.[23] Thirteen of them were serving life without parole at the time of the interview, while eight had de facto life sentences.

The second body of data came from interviews I conducted with twenty-seven prison staff with a wide range of responsibilities: custody staff, counselors, medical professionals, medical administrators, and mental health professionals. Staff were selected primarily because their responsibilities put them in a position to recognize the challenges their institutions will face as larger numbers of their populations age and decline. Staff interviews averaged about an hour in length. Each interview reviewed the staff member's obligations, his or her work with life-sentenced prisoners, and his or her assessments of the present and future challenge those prisoners pose to the interviewee's institution.

Each of these interviews was transcribed by an undergraduate research assistant.[24] Those transcriptions were then coded for persistent themes. Although the work would be richer if it included participant observation, such access was not available. The interview data, however, are sufficiently rich—and the themes across them sufficiently consistent—that I am confident in the analysis that follows.

Each of the two prisons houses both medium- and minimum-security prisoners. One is the Washington State Reformatory.

Built in 1910, it is the second-oldest prison in the state. Constructed decades before the Americans with Disabilities Act, it is by no means designed for the mobility impaired. Its cells are small and cramped, its stairs numerous. Those who need a wheelchair or walker can almost never be housed there. Exceptions can be made for inmates who need dialysis services. This prison is rare for housing a dialysis unit, and thus some accommodations can be made for those who need that service. For the most part, however, if a Washington State Reformatory prisoner cannot move about and engage in self-care, he must be transferred to another prison.

The second is the Twin Rivers Unit. It was built in 1984 and was designed with greater attention to mobility issues. Each of its four living units has two levels, so those who cannot navigate stairs can be housed on the ground floor. The facility's grounds are sloped but contain no stairs, so prisoners who use wheelchairs can move from building to building. Some of the cells are ADA-compliant, although few are large enough to house a wheelchair. To be housed at this site, then, a mobility-impaired prisoner must be able to move into and around his cell without the use of a wheelchair.

Both prisons are considered reasonably desirable. Part of this is due to their proximity to the Seattle metropolitan area, where many prisoners' families live. Also, each prison has a larger than average number of programs led by outside volunteers, a decided amenity. In addition, the Seattle area boasts the region's best medical facilities, which are frequently used by residents in each prison.

Because the prisons are favored, lifers there possess a fairly strong incentive to stay out of trouble for fear of being transferred to a worse facility.[25] But neither facility can accommodate prisoners whose physical well-being deteriorates past a certain point. That there are no obvious refuges for elderly, debilitated prisoners is one of the many challenges facing prison systems increasingly overflowing with lifers.

RECONSIDERING RETRIBUTION

What follows is an empirically anchored critique of life sentences. My data show that America's reliance on excessive punishment merits reconsideration. As I review that data, I provide a largely implicit critique of those philosophies of punishment that seemingly provide support for the increase in life sentences. To help readers best evaluate my arguments, I wish to make explicit both this philosophical critique and my own philosophical commitments.

As has been widely noted, philosophies of punishment are commonly split into two camps. One is described as retribution or retributivism. Here, the impulse is to ensure that the convicted wrongdoer faces a punishment that provides recompense for the societal injury represented by the crime. The severity of the punishment is, ideally, calibrated to the harm of the offense. In this way, the punishment is backward-looking: it assesses the damage caused by the past illegal act and imposes the requisite sentence.[26]

The other punishment approach is described as utilitarian or consequentialist. Here, punishment is forward-looking. It pursues a future goal—a reduction in criminality. Utilitarian philosophies notably differ on how that goal should best be achieved. Rehabilitation is designed to change convicts so thoroughly that they disfavor future crime. With deterrence, people hope that the threat and experience of punishment provide disincentives to any further wrongdoing. And incapacitation makes criminal behavior impossible, at least outside prisons.

The rise of mass incarceration was driven, in part, by a widespread skepticism about rehabilitation and its associated indeterminate sentences. Although rehabilitation was embraced in the 1950s and 1960s throughout the United States, by the mid-1970s there was concern about whether it was effective.[27] Concerns also arose about sentences without fixed lengths. This practice of indeterminate sentencing was justified because it ostensibly provided an incentive for prisoners to engage in rehabilitative services, the better to earn a shorter punishment. Yet such sentences were criticized for giving criminal justice officials too much discretion in determining the actual amount of time served.[28] As a result, prisoners could serve sentences of dramatically different lengths for committing similar crimes.

These critiques led to the increased adoption of determinate sentences. If rehabilitation did not appear to work, and if indeterminate sentences led to unjustified disparities in punishments, then fixed sentences were a logical alternative. Although determinate sentences can be justified by both deterrence (certainty of sentence length should discourage future crime) and incapacitation (the public is guaranteed protection for a definite period of time), they arguably earn their greatest support via the logic of retribution.[29] Most notably, retribution can be said to generate more fair sentences, because it entails calibrating the punishment to the nature of the criminal wrong.[30] Indeed, retribution is commonly encapsulated by a pithier and more accessible term—*just deserts*. This is meant to imply that criminals get sentences that are essentially their due, given the damage generated by their actions. This concern with fairness, coupled with retribution's long-standing historical significance, has made it a favored philosophy of punishment in the contemporary era.[31]

Yet retribution is vulnerable to criticism. Three principal critiques interest me. One is the difficulty of actually determining desert. Although the principle of just deserts makes intuitive sense, it proves challenging in practice to decide just how much punishment a given criminal offense deserves. As a result, it is hard to attain the equality in sentencing that is ostensibly one of retribution's main attributes.[32] A second concern is related to the first. Because retribution provides no obvious means to determine appropriate sentences, there is an ever-present danger that punishments can become more harsh. Without a strong check on the retributivist impulse, longer and longer punishments can emerge. Indeed, the rise of life sentences in the United States can be seen as one result of this tendency.[33] Finally, retribution's backward-looking orientation provides little consideration for what occurs after sentencing. Retribution thus provides neither any guidance about how to construct ideal practices of punishment nor any means to assess and respond to the changes that prisoners often undergo.

Despite these reasonable critiques of retribution, it is senseless to expect its demise. Its historic legacy is too entrenched, its moral wellsprings too deep.[34] Better, then, to isolate an approach to retribution that enables a recognition of the type of thoroughgoing change that easy keepers and others achieve. To do this, it helps to recognize that retribution is indeed fundamentally anchored in morality. As Mackie notes, retribution has an "immediate, underived moral appeal or moral authority."[35] Whether such moral immediacy is universal might be debatable, but the durability of retribution is likely connected to its moral underpinnings. However, if claims about retribution rest significantly on moral grounds, then other moral considerations must be allowed into discussions of punishment. Mercy, for instance, is also a morally anchored and notably durable justice tradition, one that deserves consideration alongside retribution. It can be justified, in part, as a brake against retribution's tendency to allow sentences to grow.[36]

In addition, a retributively based sentence can be understood as a form of communication. A punishment renders a moral lesson—about the unfairness of any benefit a criminal may attain through wrongdoing, about the need to restore the moral worth of a crime's victim, about the imperative to reinforce the collective consciousness of society.[37] A punishment is thus a message from the state imposing the sentence, to the convicted criminal. But communication can occur in the other direction, as well. A convicted criminal can recognize the moral harm of his actions and build a new life in response. In this way, as R. Anthony Duff notes,[38] a retributionist message can be both backward- and forward-looking. A sentence can communicate a moral message about the wrong of a criminal offense, but it can simultaneously encourage a convicted criminal to recognize that wrong and to repent for it through a personal transformation.[39]

In the pages that follow, I show that such transformations are common among easy keepers. In my view, no morally grounded theory of punishment can legitimately ignore this truth. Further, recognizing this truth does not mandate an abandonment of retribution. Crimes are moral wrongs and, thereby, can warrant a punishment, as retributionists assert. Punishments are thus necessarily symbolic messages expressed in recognition of the harm inherent in a crime. Yet it does not diminish the retributionist rationale to recognize that such messages are often heard by those who are convicted of crimes and frequently used as motivations for thoroughgoing change. In fact, if retribution is essentially about using punishment to restore a societal equilibrium disrupted by a crime, such a rebalancing is best achieved when convicts fundamentally transform themselves.[40] There seems no better way for them to pay their debt to society.[41]

For this reason, rehabilitation can be seen as a handmaiden to retribution. Or, put better, rehabilitation can be the means to most effectively realize retribution. The easy keepers I interviewed would likely not only agree with this argument but also hold up their own lives as illustrative examples.

OVERVIEW OF THE BOOK

I endeavor in what follows to illuminate the challenges facing life-sentenced prisoners, as well as the impressive degree to which those men meet those challenges. I also endeavor to explain what challenges they pose to the institutions that house them, particularly as they age and decline. In the process, I throw into relief many of the perhaps unintended consequences of the hyperpunitive policies that have intoxicated American politicians for too long.

Chapter 1 traces how the men I interviewed adapted to their life sentences. As I show there, this adaptation was commonly not a simple process, especially for those who entered prison at a young age. Over time, however, the men I interviewed had become more inured to their sentences and found viable coping strategies. For many, this transformation was part of a general maturation, one in which they came to see themselves as existing within a web of interdependent relations and as possessing some responsibility for the welfare of others. Their transition was also a sensible adaptation to their environment: becoming an easy keeper was a means to make their lives as bearable as possible.

Chapter 2 casts a sober eye on the realities of life-sentenced prisoners. Even if many lifers become surprisingly well-adapted and civic-minded, they do so despite monumental challenges. I chart these challenges to make two key points. The first is that, given the important role they play in stabilizing prisons, lifers deserve more support, respect, and opportunities than prisons commonly supply them. The second is that their positive social orientation merits greater attention from those who evaluate prisons and punishment policy. To become an easy keeper is a remarkable accomplishment, one worthy of greater recognition.

Chapter 3 looks at these issues from the perspective of prison staff. Like prisoners, prison staff are underresourced and under-appreciated. While they vary in their level of skill and profes-sionalism—as do workers in any large institution—prison staff themselves face considerable challenges, particularly in caring for declining prisoners. I use the chapter to review these chal-lenges and the various and often improvised strategies staff adopt to meet them. A growing population of lifers will only make pris-ons harder to manage effectively. This is yet another reason why the ubiquity of life sentences deserves reconsideration.

Chapter 4 centers on this need for reconsideration. There, I review the book's analysis for its key lessons and then use that analysis to mount a wide-ranging critique of life sentences. The concerns are wide and notable. Taken together, these criticisms of life sentences suggest the need for a broader, more inclusive, and more rational public conversation about punishment in the United States.

We need, in short, to make it much harder to keep people so easily.

CHAPTER ONE

Becoming Easy

Four months after his eighteenth birthday, Leonard clubbed an elderly neighbor to death as part of a robbery. He was convicted of aggravated murder and sentenced to life without parole.

When I first met him, he was fifty-one and in his twenty-fifth year of residence at the Washington State Reformatory. Soft-spoken and articulate, he talked openly about the person he was when first incarcerated. He was, in his terms, a "real knuckle-head," focused entirely on his own needs: "I was real selfish. Wanted to do everything my way. Which was why I was in prison. So, I got a lot of write-ups in the beginning. In the beginning, it was rough. I was in and out of the hole for various reasons."[1] This selfish orientation, he said, changed rather suddenly one day when he was twenty-four:

> The change came from inside of me, and that's what happened for me. I can't explain it. It was just—I know when it was, it was 1988. I was smoking a joint in the yard. I was smoking cigarettes at the time. I entered this Iron Man contest in the yard, where you had to run across the yard and do all these different things and, hopefully,

make it back to finish the whole thing. Well, I did it, and it just about killed me. I was so out of shape from smoking and doing the marijuana, all that kind of stuff. After the race, I just kind of sat back in the yard looking around, watching everybody do their thing. From that point forward, I decided, I wasn't going to do anything like that anymore. It was an eye-opener for me. Since that time, I have never smoked a cigarette or any marijuana. That was my last year that I got write-ups. I'm not a perfect guy, don't get me wrong, but my life has changed since '88.

In his account, what occurred was simple: "I think that I just grew up. I finally—I grew up. It took me until I was twenty-four years old to realize that and grow up and start doing the right thing." For Leonard, growing up meant focusing on "things that are good," most notably steady employment and caring family relations.

His maturity, he said, was keyed to his transcending his selfish nature: "I just didn't care about other people. I just cared about myself, what I could get for me. Everything was self-centered like that. That was the cause of it. When I committed my crime, I didn't think about the consequences or who I was hurting or anything like that. I just wanted some money. So, I didn't really think about that kind of stuff. It was just all about me. Me, me, me. But then I realized it really wasn't about me, and change started happening." Part of the change described by Leonard involved the work he does for others, most notably the members of his family. He proudly mentioned his marriage of twenty years and his parenting of his four adopted children, which he tried his best to accomplish from prison. He also noted his artwork that he donated to charities, and his work building frames for housing that will go to the impoverished. And, like other lifers, he mentioned the mentoring he provides to younger inmates. From his perspective, he was, as a lifer, part of an established and influential group in prison. As "easy keepers," they provided advice to youngsters and stability to the institution as a whole:

> LEONARD: They intervene between people that are getting ready to fight. Or they talk people out of the drugs. They talk people into going to school or programming. Getting a job. Getting them off the yard. A lot of the guys, they just like to go to the yard all day. That's all they do, just lay around the yard and go to breakfast, lunch, and dinner. They don't do anything else. Their whole day is about recreation. A lot of the lifers try to get them focused on at least one class or a program of some type. Getting more involved in the library. Going to church. Things like that.
>
> HERBERT: Why do you think they do that?
>
> LEONARD: Because I think they see a lot of what people are doing in here, the younger guys. I think they see a lot of themselves when they were younger, and they know where they ended up. I think that a lot of people struggle with that and want to do what they can to make sure that somebody else doesn't end up in the same position. That's what I believe. I've asked a lot of people about it, and they've said—not in those exact words— that's what they're doing.

For his part, Leonard struggles with the reality of his sentence and with his belief that only a change in law will prevent him from dying in prison. He copes as well as he can through adherence to a simple credo: "I've shed a lot of tears over the years, over being in prison. A lot. I still do. You never know when you're going to do something that somebody else is seeing you do, that you don't even realize, that may change their life. By doing the right thing. So I'm always trying to think I'm being watched by somebody, and always doing something. I just try to do the right thing. I do."

BECOMING AN EASY KEEPER

Although Leonard's degree of self-understanding is unusual, his story is not. The themes he highlights—a general maturation, a recognition that his actions have consequences, a desire to better those around him, a need to retain hope—are ones echoed regularly by life-sentenced prisoners. Many of the lifers I met could describe when and how they became easy keepers. They regularly referenced the same signposts in their maturation process.

Looked at one way, the transitions Leonard describes are nothing special: most humans mature with age. Yet such transitions are not easily accomplished in prison environments, where much more could be done to foster personal growth. I use chapter 2 to document the impediments that are part of everyday prison life. For now, I wish to highlight the significant social accomplishment represented by those personal transformations that regularly occur for lifers like Leonard.

At the age of fifty-one, and with the benefit of hindsight, Leonard can see the pivotal moment when he recognized the need to make some fundamental changes. Although the interviewees never described the exact same progression, there were consistencies across their stories. Many described a general maturation through which they gained a new perspective on themselves and their social relations. Part of this transformation included a recognition that they were not isolated individuals but instead were situated in interdependent relations with others. Like Leonard, they recognized that maintaining a highly individualized focus, perhaps a selfish one, was a too-constricted approach to life. Better to see themselves not as social atoms but as members of social groups. Key for many prisoners was an acknowledgment of the impacts of their conviction and incarceration on members of their families. From this recognition of interdependency came another: that if they necessarily acted in ways that affected others, they could act as a force for good rather than harm. This meant, in daily practice, that many lifers sought to improve the circumstances of those around them. Most commonly, lifers focused on younger prisoners with fixed release dates. Partly owing to a sense of altruism, but also to a desire to atone for their past offenses, many lifers seek to mentor in hopes that their younger brethren will not return to prison when released.

It is not my goal here to explain with any precision just why these transformations occur. There is now a large and rich literature on the factors that lead criminal offenders to desist from wrongdoing, which I do not wish to exhaustively review or arbitrate here.[2] I do, however, take considerable inspiration from the work of Shadd Maruna and like-minded others, who focus on the importance of self-narrative to the process of personal change.[3] The shift away from a past of criminal offenses, Maruna argues, is significantly anchored in the development of a new story about oneself. Importantly, that story can include prior wrongdoing but also a future of greater promise and purpose. Maruna's emphasis on narrative helps make sense of the interviews I analyze here, particularly his focus on how ex-offenders often develop a "redemptive script." This emphasis on redemption allows them to construct a new self-image, one that uses their past wrongdoing as a platform upon which to build a better self.[4] Notably, this better self is often focused on generative projects like mentoring and counseling.[5] As I describe below, such projects were frequently essential to lifers' sense of purpose.

Importantly, my findings about personal changes within the lifer population are consistent with other, similar, interview-based studies.[6] Indeed, the consistency of these findings is striking. Like others who interviewed prisoners with life or otherwise long sentences, I found a group of individuals who were largely well-adjusted, who created few problems for prison staff, and who worked to improve the communities of which they were a part.[7] This clearly suggests that lifers very commonly resist the temptation to give up on themselves and descend into lassitude and depression.[8] Easy keepers, in other words, are common.[9]

That so many lifers become easy keepers should not, however, minimize the significance of the accomplishment. Many lifers, particularly those who were incarcerated at a young age, come to recognize that a more mature approach to life is in their best interest. This maturation is, for many, closely connected to a recognition that they necessarily possess interdependent relations with others and, thus, unavoidably affect other people. This growing realization of interdependency is significant in its own right, but it also births an important corollary—that they can influence others positively instead of negatively. This, in turn, generates various efforts by lifers to improve the circumstances of others, most critically the younger prisoners with whom they live. These altruistic efforts have the added benefit of enabling lifers to retain some form of hope, which they all indicated was critical for their well-being.

The route to becoming an easy keeper is thus fairly well-worn, with some consistent markers for those who travel it. This is not to suggest that passing along the route is itself easy. It is not, as I emphasize in chapter 2. For now, the question is: how does "easy" become possible?

"IT WAS LIKE A CLICK": MATURATION IN THE LIFE-SENTENCED PRISONER

Rudy got a life-without-parole sentence while still a teenager for his involvement in the murder of a family of four. When he first entered prison, he was so scared that he sought the protection of a prison gang based on his ethnicity. His gang involvement, he said, meant that he engaged in frequent violence, which resulted in several trips to isolation.[10] He developed what he described as a well-earned reputation as someone willing to fight and, with it, some measure of prestige. But, with time, he reconsidered:

> At that time, I was getting older—I was more in my twenties, early twenties—and little by little things started. I started to see the outlook on everything. I started seeing everything for what it was. At the age of twenty-five, it was like a click *[snaps fingers]*. Literally, I was walking by one day and just *[snaps fingers]*—it felt like a click. And [with] that little click, I started to realize: "Wait a minute." My eyes opened up. From that time, I started realizing, "Man, a lot of the stuff I'm doing is really stupid." Like, there's some situations where I could let go of the issue instead of making it bigger than it has to be. And I started noticing this from the age of twenty-five until now. I started realizing a lot of this stuff really just is stupid. It's young, dumb stuff, and I don't need that no more.

As a result of his new outlook, Rudy said, he began to avoid violence. Unsurprisingly, his disciplinary record changed, as well.

> This year, I'll be thirty-seven. And if you ever looked at my record, you will see from the first ten-something years I was very violent. And then, from every year after that, little by little, I would go to work, I wouldn't even fight that year. I went a whole year—no fights, no nothing, no problems. I've got almost three, four, years

now, almost, without getting any major infractions. I've grown up. I didn't like the way I acted back in those days. But that's what adults do. I became an adult after a while.

Like Leonard, Rudy described a seemingly sudden realization in his midtwenties that his approach to life was shortsighted. While his interest in a gang's protection made sense when he was young and vulnerable, with age he saw the harm he was doing to himself with his violent ways.[11]

Rudy's story is common among those who receive a life sentence while young.[12] If sent to prison underaged and vulnerable, many of them ally themselves with prison gangs. This decision commits the individual to frequent bouts of violence. When incidents occur between different gangs, all members are expected to enter the fray. Even if fighting is an infraction and leads to trips to solitary confinement, gang members must display their loyalty in this fashion. Like Rudy, however, many begin to recognize the ultimate futility of these dynamics.

Victor, for example, was also willing to use violence to demonstrate his commitment to his gang. As he put it, "Yeah, I was young, crazy, willing to do whatever. I was ready to get the next guy and everything. Basically, it was a surviving skill. I embraced it because I had to embrace it."

With time, Victor realized he might benefit more by disassociating from his gang and the petty violence it required him to commit:

Eventually, I got older and got tired of fighting people for real stupid, pathetic things, like: "Oh, he crossed the line," or "He used the wrong phone." I didn't agree with that, because it upset me. And people didn't like those points of view; they didn't like a lot of stuff. So, at the end I said, "I'm done. I want to do me, I want to worry about me and my family. I don't want to worry about: 'Hey, that guy is no good, somebody has to go beat him up.'" That's not me. I could care less about their problems; I have my own problems.

Although another prisoner, Melvin, was never gang-affiliated in prison, he mimicked Leonard and Rudy in undergoing a seemingly sudden transformation. Involved in the trade and use of methamphetamines, Melvin was convicted of aggravated murder at the age of thirty and was sentenced to life without parole. Once in prison, he spiraled quickly into a depression that led to a suicide attempt. Shortly thereafter, he had an epiphany: "It's hard to explain, it's really hard to explain. But it was like: everything that was bad and all the hurt that I had, it had left. Something had clicked. I realized that what I was doing was not going to help my kids, wasn't gonna help my family, wasn't gonna help my mom and dad, wasn't gonna help me. And then I just started building on myself. Realizing that even though I was in prison, it didn't have to be bad. I could still make things good."

Leonard, Rudy, and Melvin thus all described a single moment when a lightbulb suddenly turned on, which led to a commitment to a new way of being. For others, this transition was not sudden but gradual. For Edgar, sentenced to life without parole owing to Washington's "three strikes" law, this turn toward a constructive life was simply a matter of fatigue. As he put it, "I'm done. I mean, it's just because I've grown up: I don't get high or mess around or do anything anymore. I'm just done *[laughs]*. I'm exhausted."

Gerald earned his life-without-parole sentence for a series of drug-related robberies. When young, he saw himself as invincible and rarely considered the consequences of his actions. He struck out in his late thirties and quickly began to see his life differently. As he put it, "I mean, it's a hell of a time to wake up, but I just kinda woke up, man. That this ain't it, this ain't it."

Whether as a sudden epiphany or a gradual shift, the process of maturation leads many lifers to begin writing a new self-narrative. They see that their prior lifestyle yielded limited benefits, that acting in their own best interests requires them to shift their focus and their priorities. This shift, for most, is anchored in the recognition that they are inextricably connected to others.

"MY BUTTERFLY EFFECT": INTERDEPENDENCY AND PRISONER CHANGE

Nate is serving a 134-year sentence for his involvement in a gang-related killing of a very young girl. At first, he denied any extensive involvement in the crime, but eventually he chose to acknowledge his wrongdoing. It was part of a general process of assuming more responsibility for his life and an acknowledgment of his ability to influence others. When asked how he had changed in prison, he answered,

> I think understanding, for the most part, that everything I do, all of my actions, have reactions. And it may not even affect me, so if I have an attitude of "Oh, I don't give a fuck," or whatever, I'm affecting someone else. Me cussing someone out might remind them of some traumatizing thing, or would ruin their day or ruin whatever else, or make them attack me, or whatever. So [in] all of my actions, I have to be completely and absolutely responsible for everything that I do—my butterfly effect, I guess. I think it made me realize that I have a lot more people to be accountable to than just me.

As John Irwin noted in his study of lifers, shifts in orientation among these prisoners are common. He used the term *awakening* to describe such a shift. According to Irwin: "Awakening begins when lifers fully appreciate that there has been something fundamentally wrong with their former behavior. They realize that *their* actions have brought them to this disastrous end."[13]

Another prisoner, Thomas, used lifers' ability to accept responsibility for the harms associated with their crimes to distinguish between easy keepers and other lifers in his prison. The latter group, in his view, consisted of those who failed to recognize their connections to others and, thus, failed to recognize the underlying harms of their past misdeeds:

> Usually those are guys, I think, that have not reconciled themselves with their own responsibility for the situation in which they live in now. Those are guys that can't look at themselves in the mirror and say, "You know what? I did this. I messed up. I need to redeem myself in some way and put my best foot forward." Just become better human beings. They don't have the ability to do that at times. If they're older, there's almost no helping them. So, there's a few of them here. Grumpy old men. Grumpy old lifers.

Irwin identified religion as the key to effecting an awakening. For those I interviewed, however, change more likely occurred when they recognized that their behavior negatively affected others, particularly their families. This was where Harold took the conversation when asked to describe the hardest component of his sentence:

> I think, for me, it was trying to wrap my mind around "forever." That's very hard to do. You know, like, I'm never leaving this place? What did I get myself into? For me, that's the hardest thing. But once I had that thought, the very next thought was how horrible this must be for my family. And that now became the bane of my existence. The effects that it has on my family. Some of my brothers and sisters don't write. They don't come up and visit. We don't talk anymore. My kid, my daughter, calls up, and sometimes I don't hear from her for like six months. She has a thirteen-year-old

daughter. I have a granddaughter that's thirteen years old that I want to see and I want to visit, and I want to be a part of her life. That's what's hard for me. Regardless of how hard it is for me, the daily life in here, for them it's immeasurable. For my daughter. For my son. For my granddaughter. My family. Birthdays and holidays and things come up that I should be there with them. Instead I'm here.

Particularly difficult for lifers is when close family members die, most notably parents or children. Those I spoke to often reconsidered their lives at such moments. This led them to regret their past behavior and to work toward a less-troublesome future. Said Jackson, "You know, losing my son in 2002 was rough; that really slapped me in the face. Of course, losing Pops wasn't easy either, and when Mom died, I just don't know."

Concern for their living family members also led many to reconsider the lives they were leading, as they increasingly recognized that prison misbehavior created negative familial consequences. Victor indicated that his desire to leave the gang lifestyle behind was driven by his love for his family. If he got into fights regularly, he knew he would spend time in solitary confinement and thereby make family visits notably more uncomfortable for all involved. When asked why he disengaged from gang activities, he said, "Because my family means more to me than anything else. A lot of people are like, 'Well, you know, you're just weak.' It has nothing to do with that. My family meant more to me than all that dumb stuff."

Critical to other lifers was a recognition of their impact on their victims.[14] Fred, for example, was a student in a course focused on restorative justice. When crime victims visited the class to discuss their experiences, Fred was deeply affected. His life sentence had been earned through Washington's three-strikes law. His third strike was for a robbery during which he brandished an unloaded weapon. Fred thought little about those he robbed, because he knew they were not endangered. But when crime victims came to his class, he reached a realization:

> A bunch of people came in, and I was listening. And I was talking to these people, and they were talking about getting burglarized, some of them, and how traumatic that was. That some son of a bitch was in their house digging through their underwear drawer. It made them uncomfortable to be in their house. And people that have been in—robbed in—banks, it fucked them up enough that it was hard for them to even go to work because they were scared. It was traumatic for them. And I never really realized that. And then I got to thinking about it: like, my God, somebody's in here pointing a gun at them. They don't know if you're gonna kill them or not, you know what I mean? That would scare the shit out of anybody, especially a woman, and that's who's usually in those positions, in banks, that work in those places. That kinda got to me.

In sum, the transition to becoming an easy keeper is part of a general maturation process, one that, importantly, involves lifers recognizing that they are necessarily connected to others, most particularly members of their families. Shifting away from self-centeredness, many lifers begin to see the web of interpersonal connections in which they are enmeshed. They recognize how their past behavior damaged those connections, and they suffer from a resulting guilt.

But matters do not end there. Rather than feeling crippled by regret, many lifers move from a recognition of interdependency to a commitment to assist others. If they will necessarily have influence on others, perhaps they can act as a beneficent force, not a harmful one.

"I CHOSE TO DO THE RIGHT THING FOR ONCE": THE OTHER-ORIENTATION OF LIFERS

For many lifers, seeing that they were anchored in interdependent relations with others sparked transformations. Many of them took a subsequent step—to become a supportive influence rather than a corrosive one. This recalibration was important to those who described any form of awakening. To grow and change implied an acceptance of obligations to others.

Charlie, for example, did something minor that he later realized was critical to his maturation. He was another prisoner who had entered a close custody institution as a teenager. Like other teens in prison, he joined a gang for protection. Part of his tough prisoner veneer was a fairly predatory stance toward any new cellmates. He viewed them largely in terms of what resources or favors he could coerce from them. This changed when he got a young cellmate with whom he began to identify:

> After a few months, I actually start liking this kid, and I remember it was his birthday. He really liked the band Tool. My buddy down the tier had cassette tapes of it, so I was like, "Hey, let me get one of those and record it for him, and I'll give it to him for his birthday." Evidently he was so shocked by that—you know, that gesture of, "Hey, somebody remembered it was my birthday," because normally you don't. It's not really something you announce. You get a lot of razz on your birthday. A lot of guys will come up and punch on you a little bit. You know, your buddies will give you a hard time; but it's not really something that you go, "Hey, it's my birthday." It's not an occasion like that; so it was a nice gesture on my part to say, "Hey, you know, happy birthday. This place sucks, but we do what we can." That was just one of those moments where it didn't really mean a lot at the time, but it was an opportunity where I chose to do the right thing for once and look out for somebody else and not me. It was almost like I took that step from being that kid, that same

kid sitting in that cell, to the guy who was kinda just trying to look after him a little bit.

Charlie was not alone in expressing an interest in assisting others. Across my interviews, lifers mentioned a desire to improve the circumstances of those around them, most notably younger prisoners with release dates. Lifers were particularly proud of their efforts to steer those youngsters in a more positive direction. For some, this involved tutoring sessions in educational settings. For others, it meant encouraging prisoners to join Alcoholics Anonymous or Narcotics Anonymous. For yet others, it meant providing informal counseling in workplace or religious settings or just in casual conversations.

Fred's crimes were all robberies done in pursuit of resources for drugs. He thereby recognized the intrinsic connection between his drug habit and his criminal career. He used this history in his efforts to counsel younger prisoners, many of whom struggled with drug problems. He was an active member of Narcotics Anonymous and commonly sought new recruits, particularly those younger prisoners whose habits mimicked his own former habits:

> I don't really know how to put it into words, but I started realizing that you only have so much time; I started recognizing that. Before, I didn't. I just kinda thought, "Fuck that, I won't even think about it." You don't want to think about it. I started thinking about that, and I wanted to make a difference. And the only way I kinda could make amends for all the shit that I've done in my life and put my family through was to try to help some of these kids in here. Because I was never much of a parent to my children. And, of course, you have regrets for that. You feel guilty about it. That's what I was dealing with. So I look at a lot of these little dummies around here like my kids. You know? I try to steer them in the right

direction. I want to help them find another way to do it. To find a life. To not end up in here sitting around talking to professors when you're sixty-one years old *[laughs]*.

This desire to steer younger prisoners was mentioned by almost all of the lifers I interviewed.[15] All of those whose criminal misbehavior was, like that of Fred, a result of drug involvement worked to persuade their younger brethren to avoid their example. Gerald, another three-striker, took a similar tack. When he got his life-without-parole sentence in his late thirties, he quickly underwent a change. As he put it, "I try to pass that on to some of these kids, man. They can't wait to get out there and get 'em a package and get out there on that corner or whatever and start sellin' dope or start hustlin'. And I be telling them, 'Man, I'll see you when you get back. If I'm still around, I'll see you when you get back.'"

Victor made a similar point, in reference to his own work seeking to counsel younger prisoners: "It's like talking to my old self."

Lifers are all too aware of the pain associated with their sentences. From this perspective, they are able to see youthful prisoners in a particular fashion—as individuals who might end up with life sentences themselves. Kent commented on this point:

Most of the lifers that are here, a lot of them get into a lot of the programs; and they try to work with the younger inmates and try to coax them so they can have a little bit better choices in their life and not keep coming back to these places. Because nobody wants to spend their life in here. It's miserable. You think of the stuff you miss out on. You miss out on your family, you miss out on everything. I've never even had a banana split in my life, I've never had lobster, I've never had a real relationship. It's all those things that you miss out on. I figure, if this could happen to me, if I could get through to one other individual—to point out that it could happen to them too, that if they don't change it could happen to them—that's all worth it.

Unlike Irwin's sample of lifers, those I interviewed rarely described religion as central to their personal transformations. William was an exception. He has a de facto life sentence, because his release date well exceeds his expected life span. His awakening occurred in a county jail where he awaited resolution of his case. At that time, he decided he would recommit to the Christian religious tradition in which he was raised. For William, this renewed embrace of religion primarily meant striving to serve others through counseling. He became a strong figure in his prison's religious community and sought to earn the trust of younger prisoners. He encouraged them to unburden themselves of their deep-seated insecurities, the better to control the emotional forces that contributed to their criminality. He understood well the underlying trauma that afflicts many inmates:

> I believe that I'm actually helping people understand themselves a lot better, because people in this atmosphere wear a lot of masks. People in this atmosphere been through a lot of abuse, sexual, all of it. I mean the list goes on and on. And they thought it was their fault rather than the other person's fault. And because they thought it was their fault, they thought they was inadequate as an individual; they went through life acting out on this, on this bad behavior that happened in their lives. Once they shared and realized—I've seen men cry on my shoulder after explaining these things to them.[16]

This was work that William found tremendously rewarding: "Nothing brings about more joy for me than to see a guy change from angry and bitter to the human being that they need to be."

Although he lacked William's religious commitment, Melvin sought to similarly influence younger prisoners. Melvin enjoyed working, and he proudly listed the range of labor assignments he had worked throughout his twenty-two years of incarceration. Besides appreciating the happiness that work provided him, Melvin liked serving as a role model for younger prisoners with whom he labored. He enjoyed demonstrating the value of hard work. He also enjoyed using the workplace setting to provide informal counseling. At the time of our conversation, Melvin was building frames for housing for low-income families. He found the work gratifying, for multiple reasons:

> Yeah, frame and hammer. I enjoy it, I do. The money—there ain't no money in it. Sometimes I make twenty bucks a month. But the kids: teachin' them, and seein' how excited they are to wanna learn. Not all of them, but there's a good group of them that are. And then I get to get in their ear about how long I've been here, and why, and how quick your life can change. So I guess the money part of it doesn't really matter. I tell Ralph out there—he's the supervisor—tell him, "If you save one, if you save one guy, it's all worth it." Not to come back with a life sentence.

As they encounter younger prisoners, then, lifers try to use their influence toward constructive ends. Lifers are aware that they are persons of some stature, and they trade on this status to try to influence younger prisoners. They adopt the role of what White terms "wounded healers": they use their experiences as moral leverage against the destructive impulses of their younger peers.[17] In the process, they construct a new self-identity as an agent of positive change.[18]

A central component of this identity reconstruction is a recalibration of the story of their lives. With much time on their hands, lifers have ample opportunity to reflect on their pasts and to look forward to some form of a future. The work that they do around the prison is part of this restructured narrative.[19] Life-sentenced prisoners do good works because of the positive impact it can generate for others, but also because they can simultaneously write a new story about themselves, one that can provide a sense of both atonement and hope.

"MAYBE THAT WILL BE SOME WAY TO GIVE BACK": ATONEMENT AND HOPE FOR LIFERS

As noted above, Melvin was sentenced to life without parole after his conviction for aggravated murder. His ability to maintain a strong connection to his family was his proudest accomplishment. He was still married after more than twenty years in prison, and was actively involved in the lives of his children and grandchildren. He also stayed employed and sought to counsel younger prisoners. He thus labored to be an asset to those with whom he was associated. But he also did so because he sought to provide some form of recompense for the crime he had committed. When asked if he felt a need to atone for his crime, he said yes, and then elaborated:

> And maybe just try to keep giving back; that's all I can do. Try to be a good person. I try to live my life in here like I would out there—family, work, and trying to give back. Is there anything that I could do to make up for that? I don't know. I honestly don't know. I would hope that maybe I'll touch that one kid or that one person in here that's maybe thinking about coming back, and [who will] think about Melvin being in prison for twenty-five years. And maybe that will be some way to give back: they won't go out there and take somebody's life and end up in here. So I guess there's a variety of different things that you hope will come out of it.

Melvin was not alone in expressing both guilt for the harm he had caused and determination to be a positive example to others. He and others hoped that their lives would thereby seem less like they were lived in vain. Dean, a father of three serving a life-without-parole sentence, remarked, "Right now, I owe my kids a lot because I wasn't there for them. And I regret every bit of it, because I haven't seen them graduate, or seen them on their birthdays. And when you talk about something that hurts me really, it is that I wasn't there for them. I can send them money, but that's not the same as me being there in person, so ... I owe them a lot, too."

Oscar had long and successful careers, first in the military and then in business, but was convicted of aggravated murder and sentenced to life without parole at the age of fifty. He likened his sentence to being on patrol "day after day after day after day. They seem to all be the same, and you do your job and keep going and know that there is going to be another day." While he maintains hope that he may earn clemency, he was in his late seventies at the time of our conversation. He could thus acknowledge the strong possibility he would die in prison. Still, he retained an interest in atonement:

> OSCAR: I try, personally try, to be realistic about it and say, "Hey, there's maybe—when I say 'the best place,' a little bit tongue and cheek—but [a place] where I can, under the circumstances, do the most good for myself and for others." Again, try and make the most out of what is there and what's available. I do that and keep going, and it sustains me.
>
> HERBERT: Why is doing good so important to you?
>
> OSCAR: Because I did bad. That's kind of a glib answer. I think doing good was always the way I was brought up. You try and do good, and you try and do your best; and I did more than slip up. So, all I can do is to move on and try and make the most out of what is there, and what is here.

Thus, many lifers spend time looking back and trying to address the guilt they feel by pursuing good works that might generate some recompense for their misdeeds. They also commonly look forward. Although their outlook for release is grim, they each said that they refuse to accept that they will, in fact, die in prison. Many of them indicated that such a fate was so debilitating that they simply could not countenance it. Gerald was adamant about his need for hope, because the alternative was unacceptable:

> If I didn't [have hope], I wouldn't even be here talking to you. For real. I mean, that's just reality. If that'd be the case, if the light ain't never gonna come on, when you don't have nothing, then you don't have nothing to lose. That's for real in the penitentiary. I'm saying that because, you know, I've known guys that have multiple murders that have been able to pass positive things on to people coming in behind them, cause I've had some of them guys pass things on to me. And they still have hope. For the most part, a lot of them still have hope. So, like I said, I truly believe that something's gonna happen. Some kinda thing, I don't know.

Many lifers were able to point to others who managed to leave prison, owing either to a successful clemency appeal or a legal development in their case. And they all could see how larger numbers of aging inmates were taxing the prison system; thus, many presumed that a shift in sentencing policy would eventually need to occur. Dean explained to me, "Yeah, well, see, the thing is, just because it says 'life without' don't mean you're never getting out. Because I know some people right now that had life without that got their time, went back to court, and they are out in the street right now. So a sentence don't mean nothing."

For many, the preservation of hope was indispensable to their ability to persevere.[20] Hope, said Melvin, is "what keeps you going." As much as they expressed satisfaction in the everyday work they did, many also viewed that work against the backdrop of a future that necessarily included a future release.[21] Nate captured this idea well:

> As the courts see it, I will be in here until death. But I can't see myself being here that long, I just cannot accept that. You know, my kids are getting grown and family members are passing away. That's when it hits you. But it has still not hit me to where I'm at a "Woe is me, what can I do?"—I just can't give in to that. You know what I mean? I've made the decision I'm gonna live as if I'm getting out, every day. Every day I have to do that.

Burt was convicted in his sixties for murdering his wife. He is set to be released in 2028, when he will be eighty-three. The Department of Corrections considers him a de facto lifer. In other words, the department believes he will die before he is released. Burt uses hope to resist this idea: "I think it's a bad mind-set to have, to think like you don't have any hope of getting out. Even though chances are not great; it gives me a chance to work on relationships and try to continue things—although I don't know. Anyway, no, I'm not a lifer, thank you very much."

This preservation of hope cannot be easy. Just as lifers can point to prisoners who were released, so too can they list those who have died in the prison hospital. Yet they so abhor such an ignominious end that they stubbornly nurture visions of a future life outside of prison.[22] The self-narrative that they reinforce daily necessarily points ahead in time. For that narrative to work, the future must include more than a glimmer of hope that release is possible, even when they acknowledge that death in prison is likely. William explained this to me:

There's times I get lonely. I had a visit a couple weeks ago from my daughter, and I bawled like a little baby out here in front because she surprised me. And I didn't want to let her go. All of those things is part of my human experience. But at the same time, do I look at that, and then go back to where I'm going and there's a feeling of despair? No. I have a feeling of hope, even though I'm sure I'll probably die in here; but I still have a feeling of hope.

CONCLUSION: "YEAH, RESILIENCE IS HUMAN NATURE, YOU KNOW"

Many prisoners sentenced to life or otherwise long sentences become easy keepers. To come to terms with their sentences commonly means, for lifers, to fundamentally restructure their lives. Acutely aware of the social losses they have suffered, and remorseful about the pain they have caused, they endeavor to be an asset and not a hindrance. Cognizant of their interdependencies, they hope to help others desist from future crime. Although banished from society as a whole, they remain enmeshed in social relations that they seek to make meaningful through generous acts of mentorship.

To acknowledge that the transition to easy-keeper status is common is not to suggest that it is simple. The shift is often a multistage process that is part ordinary maturation and part daily dedication to constructive pursuits. It also often involves both an inmate's reckoning with a misbegotten past and his acceptance of responsibility for the pain associated with his crimes. Burdened by guilt, cognizant of how their families have suffered, terrified of the failure that death in prison could represent, many lifers spend their days rededicating themselves to a more purposeful and meaningful life. In the process, they demonstrate a notable degree of strength and determination. As Nate put it, "Yeah, resilience is human nature, you know."[23]

The strength of this resiliency is even more remarkable when one considers in greater detail the challenges that daily prison life poses to anyone who embraces redemption. I use chapter 2 to catalogue and assess some of those challenges.

CHAPTER TWO

Being Easy Isn't Easy

Two of the hardest moments in prison for Melvin occurred when each of his parents died. Not simply grief-stricken, Melvin was also filled with shame: "Just to know where I was when they passed, to know that I was in prison. My mom—that her son was in prison and was never gonna get out. And how much that had to have hurt her."

Still, Melvin was granted permission to attend her funeral. The suit and tie he was allowed to wear enabled him to blend into the crowd. That clothing option was not afforded him when his father later died:

> They wanted me to wear orange. When I went to my mom's [funeral], I got to wear my clothes. They wrote a report; couldn't have went any better. But when my dad died, my counselor decided that, because I had life without, I should wear orange. I didn't want to disrespect my dad. And I told them, "This isn't about me, this is his day. I don't want the attention on me. I don't want to come into this in orange, have everybody taking the attention onto me." I tried to explain that to this counselor. He said, "You have life without parole, I don't care." So I told him, "I can't go." My dad was

ex-marine, tough. I said, "I can't do that. I can't. I can't." And still, it hurts me. That I wasn't there. It's one of the things that I hope and pray [for]: that I can get out, so I can at least go. I've told him sorry a million times, but I wanna go see him. But it's hard.

Leonard conveyed a similar sense of shame, which he had felt when he left the prison for a medical issue:

> I went down to a doctor's appointment not too long ago. I was so embarrassed getting out of the car and walking into the hospital, and all the people staring at me and stuff. I was just humiliated. The feeling that I had of being fifty-one years old and being shackled like that, it was just—it was hard. I can't even describe how hard it was. I was ashamed. I was. I actually had to tell the doctor that I had been in prison for over thirty years, because in my mind, at least, it showed him that I didn't commit a crime at the age of fifty-one. You see what I'm saying? I had to say that because—I don't know—I just had to. It's hard. Leaving here tonight and going back to my room and getting locked up. Not being trusted enough to walk down the tier without being watched. It's just humiliating.

For his part, Burt was flabbergasted when prison staff struggled to recognize his status as a dentist. When mail addressed to him included the appellation of "Doctor," the prison refused it. Burt took the symbolic message hard: "Yeah. You do not have a title. Other than 'offender.' So, that's part of that thing. It was a rude awakening—not that I felt like I should have any special privileges. But you still look to utilize what skill you have and to be productive."

THE CHALLENGES OF BEING EASY

In chapter 1, I described the processes through which easy keepers attain that status. Although many lifers pass through those stages, they can at no point forget how society scorns them. The moments that Melvin, Leonard, and Burt describe are especially poignant, but they illustrate the generalized stigma that enshrouds lifers. It is notable that so many of them manage this and other challenges on the way to becoming easy keepers.

Prisons are not easy environments. Indeed, there is a large literature on prison life that emphasizes the pains, even harms, that it causes inmates.[1] Part of the pain of prison life stems from the symbolic slights that Melvin, Leonard, and Burt emphasize in their stories. In numerous ways, prisoners are reminded daily of their degraded status.[2] They are subject to multiple deprivations and expected to obey myriad rules that are not always clearly explained or consistently enforced. They encounter staff who are not always respectful or fair.[3] Their mobility is limited by strict prison rules. Their ability to develop trusting, supportive friendships with other inmates is constrained by the informal rules that often govern prison social relations. Their capacity to maintain outside networks is hampered by factors of time, distance, and financial resources. Their desires to enroll in programs and receive job assignments are often unmet, owing to administrators' preference to prioritize such opportunities for prisoners who will be released. Their hope to earn a decent salary and thereby provide some form of financial support to their loved ones is constrained by limitations on work opportunities and by prison pay scales that are scanty at best. And their wish to atone for their crimes in the most direct and satisfying way possible is thwarted by rules that prevent contact with their victims.

I review these constraints primarily to accentuate the accomplishment that becoming an easy keeper represents. The inherent deprivations of prison life place notable burdens on prisoners in their conduct of daily affairs. That so many overcome these burdens to construct lives that are purposeful and positive reveals a resilience, drive, and creativity that deserve wider understanding and consideration. We would do well to recognize that being easy is by no means easy.

I start my analysis by focusing on the social relations in which prisoners are enmeshed, in order to draw attention to three groups with whom lifers interact—prison staff, outside family and friends, and fellow prisoners. Prisoners can describe considerable challenges in each case that confront their efforts to forge beneficent relations. The obstacles that lifers face in their efforts to find work, enroll in programs, or otherwise find constructive outlets for their energies mean that, as eager as they are to develop their human capital and to improve their communities, lifers commonly cannot find sufficient opportunities to do so. In their efforts to provide strong and satisfying forms of recompense for their crimes, their fullest hopes for redemption are thereby rebuffed, in their view. The particular way that retribution is defined in American punishment policy inhibits their ability to repair the damage caused by their transgressions.

Taken together, these considerations underscore the need to reconsider punishment policies. The American polity would be better served if lifers' ability to become easy keepers was more broadly recognized and their efforts to redeem themselves more openly celebrated. Certainly, the attainment of easy-keeper status can be better appreciated if we recognize the constraints under which lifers operate. The difficulties inherent in a life sentence make their efforts to find meaning and purpose all the more impressive.

"THIS BACKDROP OF VITRIOL
BETWEEN KEEPERS AND THE KEPT":
THE CHALLENGES OF PRISONER-STAFF RELATIONS

Prisoners and prison staff struggle to develop cordial and respectful relations even in the best of circumstances. Part of this is due to a fundamental purpose of a prison—to protect society from unwanted, sometimes violent criminals. Because of this, staff members are necessarily preoccupied with security. Although escapes are rare, they bring especially unwelcome attention to any institution, as do riots or other forms of significant violence. Staff are thus vigilant about maintaining order, in no small part to help ensure their own personal security and that of their fellow workers. It is easy to comprehend why they take refuge in regularized routines that enable them to monitor prisoners' actions as effectively as possible.[4] The liberties of prisoners are sacrificed in the name of public safety and institutional security.

For many prisoners, however, these restrictions on liberty are less bothersome than what they perceive to be a lack of respectful relations. This complaint was most commonly expressed by older prisoners, particularly those who had been incarcerated for many years. Burt commented on this:

> BURT: One of the issues that we have constantly is this backdrop of vitriol between keepers and the kept. I think there's an adversarial definition there. We're the bad guys, they're the keepers, they're the ones protecting society. They use that a lot, and I don't give much credence to it. But that's the way they see themselves, and they don't think we deserve much at all. Some of them do; a lot of them don't. A few of them seem halfway cordial, or at least not surly, in how they carry it out, but there's so much emphasis now on not answering certain questions, not befriending any inmate.

HERBERT: For fear they're going to be manipulated?

BURT: Yeah. I think that's really drummed into them now in their training.

As Burt indicates, he believes the social distance that staff maintain derives from a concern about potential manipulation. Deceitful prisoners might use personal closeness to persuade staff to do them special favors, such as provide help with the illicit trade of goods like drugs or even with an escape attempt. Older prisoners indicated that this fear of manipulation was a newer phenomenon, which led them to suspect that a shift in officer training had occurred in the recent past. Many of these older prisoners suggested that staff had once been more generally respectful. In their accounts, veteran staff members were typically more cordial than newer ones.

This widespread belief by prisoners, that staff cannot consistently construct respectful relations, was commonly referenced as a pervasive irritant. Said Victor,

> The hardest part of being in here for life is that the COs look down on me. They think that they're better than me because I'm a prisoner.[5] And in reality, it's like—I don't know, man. They think that if I was to have a heart attack here, or something bad was to happen to me, they wouldn't do nothing. And that's not good; I'm human. If I see somebody getting hurt or whatever, I'm going to try to help them. I just get that vibe from them. Not all of them, but there is a lot of them.

As Victor indicates, prisoners were able to make distinctions between staff whom they thought were respectful and those who were not. But all of them were frustrated that staff acted in ways that reinforced the stigma of criminal conviction.

In addition to their complaints about these symbolic slights, many lifers also expressed disappointment at how the lack of respect influenced their prison community. William had worked as a uniformed officer himself before his conviction. One of his jobs had been to escort jailed prisoners to and from their court appearances. In his experience, this task was made easier when he treated his charges with respect:

> Not be a friend, but really understand and [show] some type of compassion, in the sense that you trust me in uniform. A patrol officer wants to gain the trust of the public. You don't know when he might need the public. But if he gained no trust, would the public be there to help him? The same principle applies in here. This is a community. And in this community, if you don't establish some kind of balance and reputation in treating all people the same, regardless of color, creed, or et cetera, you gonna have a difficult time.[6]

Burt seconded this assessment. From his perspective, staff worries about prisoners would be reduced if the social distance between them were lessened, or if staff took greater steps to ensure better handling of prisoners: "There would be a lot less reason for any fear if we were treated more humanely and decently."

William would like officers to take matters even further. He believes that they should take a more active role in monitoring the well-being—both physical and emotional—of the prisoners in their charge. In his view, if custody staff were aware of the activities in which prisoners were engaged, they could provide greater reinforcement of prisoner efforts at self-change. That was not the pattern, he indicated: "Interpersonal skills are not the forte of these people around here."

One manifestation of this lack of effective communication, according to many lifers, was the inability or unwillingness of prison staff to justify their decisions. Prison rules are simultaneously numerous and inconsistently enforced. As just one example, prisoners are not allowed to loan or give any item to a peer. This rule is designed to limit the possibility of one prisoner gaining undue influence over another because of any outstanding debts. Yet prisoners borrow from each other incessantly. Many lifers indicated that they would always provide food to an inmate they knew was hungry. Thus, any prison staff member who is aware of such behavior is placed in an unenviable position: he must decide whether to enforce a regulation when it is clear that no great harm is occurring. This is just one instance, of many, where staff possess discretionary authority.

For lifers, this reality is trouble enough, but matters are worsened when they receive no justification for any particular decision. This was especially true when a prison rule was difficult for the prisoner to understand in the first place. An outside friend of Thomas's sent a letter that did not make it past the prison mailroom. As he described the incident to me, he revealed a more pervasive frustration: "I had a letter and an envelope rejected because of light blue paper. Well, I have no idea what that amounts to. And I've tried writing kites and crying, "Oh, what does this mean?"[7] And I've kind of given up. It beat me down to a point where I'm not going to go back to that again, you know?"

Another common issue for prisoners, and especially for lifers, concerned staff treatment of their property. Cell searches are a part of prison life. Even if prisoners grudgingly accept that such searches will occur, they are simultaneously worried about the treatment of their possessions. This is an especially critical issue for lifers, as Rudy explained:

> In my own house, that's me. That's not your property right there. Everything in that house is just me. This is my home, I'm gonna be living in it for however long I'm sentenced to. Whether that's forever or sixty years from now, this is what I own. Every little thing

in that house is [of] value to me. Every little thing is precious. We don't have much. We have very little, so every little thing counts to us. A guy who's only been here three years, and you tear a picture of his, he's not gonna care, because he's going home. But [for] a guy who's doing life without, or doing tons of time, every little thing counts. That's the difference between us and everybody else. That's how our mentality is right now. That's why most of the guards, the smart ones, the older ones who've been working here for five or ten or twenty years, they will not mess with my personals.

Rudy expected officers to understand the very limited frame of his existence and how that limitation magnified the meaning of each of his possessions. An officer who failed to understand that was, in his view, not worthy of respect.

For Melvin, a good staff member was easy to spot: it was someone who treated inmates humanely and looked past the crimes for which they had been convicted. When asked to describe the characteristics of a good prison officer, Melvin did not hesitate:

> Respect. I think the big thing is respect. That they treat you how they want to be treated. They treat you like a human; they don't treat you like you done something wrong. They're treating you how you act. And that's basically what a lot of us want: just treat me how I treat you. And those are the ones that [are] not in here to enforce every rule. If I give somebody a soup, they're not gonna write you up for this soup. They're not trying to nitpick you; they understand that you're doin' time. They're a lot easier to get along with. And the biggest thing is respect.[8]

Although this was less a function of the actions of staff with whom they interacted regularly, lifers made frequent mention of the fact that much of their income was garnished for various reasons.[9] As a consequence, their already meager wages left them unable to meet many of their basic needs.[10] With limited funds, they could not afford as many items from the commissary as they might like. In addition, any medical visit required a payment of four dollars. Costs also accompanied the use of such facilities as the weight room and the music room. This led to common complaints about the fundamental legitimacy of the institution. Said Dean,

> What is really a tragedy in my mind is in how DOC [the Department of Corrections] operates. If you gonna incarcerate people, they shouldn't be charged money to purchase just basic things, like toothbrush, toothpaste, soap. I never heard of this in my life, where you, as a prisoner, [who] has lost a great deal of your ability to earn money, are being charged for basic things that you need. And every toothbrush a man gets, every tube of toothpaste or soap, builds the debt. I don't know how that is not cruel and unusual punishment. We don't get a lot of free anything here. I have never in my life understood: how can a prison system charge you for your basic needs of incarceration? I don't understand that.

One of their basic needs was, of course, health care. Although many lifers could point to positive experiences with the medical and mental health staff, others complained about the difficulty of getting health care in a straightforward fashion. Some complained of extensive nerve damage, others of difficulty getting a sleep apnea machine that they felt they needed. Some mentioned the inability to get high-quality crowns for their teeth, and they suffered from pain because they did not want to undergo an extraction without an adequate replacement. Burt indicated that if his lawyer son had not intervened, he might never have received a lifesaving heart procedure. Many lifers have a strong sense that their medical woes are not taken seriously, and they noted that the postponement of care was a common practice. And all griped about the four-dollar co-pay, which they knew taxed many of their less-affluent peers. With many health issues, said Kent, "you kind of suffer through it." For this reason, some lifers fear that their needs are left unmet because of an unwillingness to invest in their long-term care.

As I discuss in more detail in chapter 3, there are constraints on the quality of care that prisoners receive, and so there is likely some merit in the lifers' complaints about health care. But it is, of course, impossible to imagine a situation where prisoners do not complain of suboptimal treatment from prison staff. The inherent restrictions on their freedom and the monotony of their routine-driven existence will inevitably generate grievances. For the lifers I interviewed, however, the larger issue was a symbolic one: that the sometimes penurious treatment they received was, they feared, indicative of the stigma of being a convict.[11] These symbolic slights were perhaps the most harmful because of the damage to the individuals' sense of self that resulted. Lifers were frustrated enough about such slights directed at themselves, but even more concerned about what they perceived to be callous treatment of their outside visitors.

Lifers understandably cherish visits. Yet some expressed guilt about subjecting their loved ones to the screening process that occurs beforehand. Visitors' clothing is scrutinized (there are numerous prison restrictions that delimit proper visitor attire), and visitors must undergo a security check. Prisoners themselves are subjected to strip searches after they see a visitor. The indignities of this situation rankled lifers, particularly those who had elderly parents. Gerald was especially impassioned on this issue:

> I might have a visit a few times here and there. But I don't wish that upon anybody, having to have their people come through here. When you got an eighty-something-year-old mother that has to take off her shoes and take off her pieces of clothing, just so the

police can fondle along [her] body and come into this environment. And there's a dignity thing to that that I don't like to put my people through. It's bad enough that I gotta take off my clothes anytime I go somewhere around here, you know. In and out to these visiting rooms, and shit like that. And they gotta look at my ass and something like that, for whatever reason.

Victor, another prisoner, got similarly heated when he mentioned the treatment of his cancer-stricken mother who came for what ended up being her last visit to him:

My mom came here, and she was under chemo. And when you are in chemo, you have to use the bathroom constantly. And she said she needed to use the bathroom; so I come and ask the CO, and he just ignores me. My mom would have crapped her pants in front of everybody, and I would have snapped. Plain and simple. That would be something worth snapping about. But they ignore you, like she's here to visit someone who don't matter. You think that they'd show respect, but they treat us like we don't exist. That's the way I took it.

The issue of the treatment of their visitors deeply affects those with life sentences, especially their ability to remain connected to family and other loved ones. Given the importance of outside relations to their well-being, many lifers referenced this issue when they discussed the challenges of their sentences.

"ONE THING WILL HAPPEN— YOUR FAMILY WILL FALL OUT WITH TIME": THE CHALLENGE OF STAYING CONNECTED

Harold was a three-striker whose final conviction involved an assault on his mother. Needless to say, his crime created perturbations within his family and led some of his siblings to repudiate him permanently. For those who chose to stay connected, the length of Harold's sentence, the distance between their homes and his prison, and the various visiting procedures meant they were decreasingly likely to visit. He was not the only lifer whom he witnessed losing touch. As he put it, "One thing will happen: your family will fall out with time."[12]

Part of this falling out involved the family deaths that inevitably occur as the years tick away. Kent was able to list those whom he had lost during his more than thirty years in prison: "I lost my father, all my grandparents—all four of my grandparents, both grandmothers and both grandfathers—my uncle, my cousin, my brother's wife, who was like a little sister to me, my sister. They keep passing away, and I don't even get to go to say good-bye to 'em. So that can be difficult." Even those who succeeded in maintaining their marriages and strong relations with their children and grandchildren recounted the substantial challenges they faced. Their family members often must travel significant distances for a visit. The visits themselves can be canceled or shortened if an incident occurs that requires a lockdown. Extended family visits are allowed only infrequently and cost ten dollars a night. Phone calls, video calls, and email are all available, but they are managed by for-profit, private carriers and thus are costly.

On top of this, even those lifers who cherish their family members and work hard to stay strongly connected acknowledge that they are often burdened by guilt. They wonder whether their family members are really well-served through involvement with someone with a life sentence. Leonard, for example, worked to be a good husband and father but recognized the challenges in doing so:

LEONARD: It's not easy. It's not easy for the kids, for my wife. It's not easy for me, because I know that they deserve a lot more than what I can give them. As I look back on my life now, you know, I wouldn't recommend somebody getting married in prison, because it's really hard. The spouse really deserves a lot more than that. If something happens right now, if my wife's in distress right now, I can't do a thing about it. She's trapped on the side of the road or—you know what I'm saying? There's just nothing I can do. It's hard.

HERBERT: But you've persevered.

LEONARD: We've persevered. Absolutely. Takes a very strong woman to stay married to somebody like me. But we've done it.

Melvin, too, struggled with guilt, knowing that, for now and for the future, he is, and will be, less able to assist his wife than he would like: "I think about my wife a lot. When she gets ready to retire, how tough is that gonna be for her by herself? I think about that stuff, and that weighs on me quite a bit too. I ask her, 'How long do you wanna do this?' and she'll tell you, 'Forever.' That's just her. So I tell her, 'Anytime you get tired of this … You've done a life sentence.'"

It was this reality that prevented Fred from ever allowing any relationship with a woman to get close to the possibility of marriage. He was unable to allow a woman to share his situation that deeply:

The couple relationships that I do still have—I would never want to put anybody through this. I know of some of my friends that are married, and they go to the trailer and all that, and that's nice. But to me, it's a really selfish thing to do, because, basically, you're making some poor woman do this sentence with you. You know, so you'll have some comfort going through. But to be honest, it's not much of a life for some poor woman to have her life revolve around this visiting room and what you've got going on in here. Especially when it's been my choice to do this to myself.

That said, lifers commonly express a fear of being alone. Death in prison is frightful enough, but just as terrifying is the quiet, lonely existence that might well precede it.[13] Melvin pointed to one individual whose fate he hoped to avoid:

> I feel for some of the guys that don't have anything. They don't have family. I wonder how do they do it. What keeps them going? That don't have anybody, don't have that wife or kids or grandkids. What keeps them going? There's a guy in there right now, he has no one. No family. He's disabled, so he has no job. He never goes outside. So he sits in his cell pretty much all day, every day, seven days a week, and has been doing that for many, many years—twelve that I know of. Used to be really active, life without, used to go out, work out, worked. And then one day—nothing. He just sits in his cell. And I don't know how he does it, not to do anything. I think about him a lot.

For lifers, then, a key challenge emerges from their strongly felt need to remain meaningfully connected to family members and other loved ones who are outside. With time, such connections often wither. Family members die, the hassles and costs of prison visits begin to mount, people move on with their lives. As Nate put it, "Time waits on no one." It is thus a considerable accomplishment that many lifers do stay connected. Similarly, it is remarkable that many lifers stay positive even as their outside connections fray and sometimes dissolve. This accomplishment is all the more notable when one considers the inherent difficulties they face in forging strong, trusting relationships with each other.

"I THINK BECAUSE IT GIVES THE IMPRESSION OF A WEAKNESS": THE SCARCITY OF TRUST IN PRISONER RELATIONS

Becoming an easy keeper requires the series of personal changes that I elaborated in chapter 1. Easy keepers mature: they learn to take the needs of others seriously, and they orient themselves toward improving their social worlds. The significance of this growth is heightened when one recognizes that prisoners struggle to develop trusting relationships with one another. Prisons are cramped spaces characterized by multiple forms of deprivation. Many prisoners, especially the young ones, are impulsive and loud. Others are predatory and will look to take advantage of anyone's perceived weaknesses. Moments for quiet, contemplative, emotionally honest conversations with a peer are hard to come by and potentially to be feared.

Charlie was fortunate to have a wife in whom he could confide. He recognized that he had to resist such emotional honesty with his peers. When asked to explain why, he said,

> I think because it gives the impression of a weakness. In prison, you don't want to show weaknesses, in an environment where if you're perceived as weak you might be the next target. I think a lot of guys don't want to open up and let other people know that they have doubts or that they are hurting for whatever reason. Guys tend to keep a lot to themselves in that manner. My wife will always ask me just normal stuff about my friends: "Well, how much time's he got?" "I don't know." Or something about them—just, I don't know. "Well, why don't you know? You're friends with him." "We just don't talk about that stuff." It's not really prison conduct, but it's just a kind of macho thing, to where we don't get all touchy-feely or explain our feelings to each other. It's not quite the environment.

The lifers I interviewed preferred to be in the medium-security facilities that housed them, rather than in the other possible prison alternatives in Washington State. Yet lifers in Washington are required to serve the first part of their sentence in a close custody institution.[14] There, survival is harder. Kent went into such a facility in his early twenties and realized that he needed to toughen up to survive: "The adage that the weak will perish is pretty true in here. You don't want to be weak in prison. And I got hard pretty quick."[15]

This tough, masculinist posture may have survival benefits, but it undercuts the capacity of prisoners to develop the close, trusting relationships that are often essential to personal growth.[16] Like Kent, Burt found himself becoming closed to others for fear of betraying an unwelcome vulnerability: "It's just too hard to create trust. And I think I talked a little bit about the paranoia that I see. I see it in myself: it's part of the system. Lack of trust, a little bit of paranoia, always not being totally truthful. And that's hard."

For Burt and others, a significant part of the issue was the younger prisoners, whom he described as loud, impetuous, and deceptive: "It's basic things like: so many thieves, so many liars—bald-faced liars. Two-faced, talk behind your back. So ... you know ... the true friendships are few and far between.... Some of their behavior does really bother me. You know, not working, not caring enough about anybody else, other than themselves."

Given the paucity of trusting relationships, many lifers indicated that personal growth was often a solo project. In an environment where vulnerability could be a danger, emotional struggles are usually borne alone.[17] Thomas described what commonly occurs when an inmate is experiencing personal difficulties: "They can turn to their friends, but really a lot of it is on them.

You know, it's something that they kind of have to struggle through. There'll be a lot of times where, if it's a really difficult struggle like that, you won't see people talking about it. It's kind of an internal fight. You might not even be aware of it other than to see them a little quieter or moodier than they normally are."

In addition to the lack of trust, the general environment of despair and hopelessness thwarts prisoner growth. Nate was among those prisoners who stressed the importance of hope in helping him maintain a positive orientation in his life. When asked if such hope was easy to maintain, he quickly answered, "No. Because it's a negative vibe everywhere you go. If movement is a minute late, you hear somebody: 'Ah, what the F this and that?' or 'Man, I bet you we [are] on lockdown,' or 'Why they trippin'?' I mean it's always negative. Never can be anything else. Or we might get out early, and it's: 'This is a trap!' It's really negative. So you have to not listen to the nay-sayers. And just keep a positive outlook."

Some lifers demonstrate a particularly high level of maturity through their capacity to empathize with those youngsters whose behavior is understandably irritating. William and Melvin, as noted earlier, were deeply focused on helping divert younger prisoners off the path of continued criminality. As they worked with younger prisoners, the two of them came to a deeper appreciation of the underlying struggles that many faced. They also endeavored to find a better nature inside their younger peers that they could reach. When William was asked to describe the most pressing challenge of his sentence, he remarked,

> I probably could say it is to be around all the hurt 24/7. If you have any kind of heart. You see young mens that can't read or write. And you see young mens that are being abused, that are being made fun of. And hear about them being raped. Every fiber in you would be

angry, particularly if you haven't lost your sense of humanity. I can tell you this from my own personal life, living in here, that I don't know of a man that is not suffering in some degree or another.

When he was asked why it was so important for him to seek to counsel younger prisoners, Melvin answered,

> I have a son. And just being here for twenty-five years. And the hurt. The tears that I've inflicted on my family. That I know that these guys are doing the same thing. Good kids. And I get to hear some of their stories, in group homes, foster homes. They've been through it. And it's too bad the DOC—that there's not something, because a lot of these kids, they want somebody to talk to. I kinda joke around with 'em a little bit. But they want somebody to talk to. And I listen. As much as I'm talking to them, I'm listening to what they're sayin'. Cause there's some really good kids. There is. There's some really, really good kids and good guys in here—that you hope will get it.

That William and Melvin have been able to develop this heightened understanding of the unaddressed hurt and trauma that surrounds them is yet another indication of their maturity, despite an environment in which trusting, open relationships are rare. The difficulty of conducting emotionally honest conversations stands as a notable impediment to personal growth and is one of the obstacles to becoming an easy keeper. This challenge is magnified by the struggles that life-sentenced prisoners often face in staying engaged with constructive activities.

"WE DON'T REALLY HAVE AN OUTLET": THE STRUGGLE TO STAY ACTIVE

Sean was a middle-aged professional who received a de facto life sentence after he murdered his wife. He had faced some serious medical issues while incarcerated, but had largely recovered from them by the time of our interview. He was active in his prison's church community and worked to stay as engaged as he could. He was significantly frustrated, however, because of his inability to come anywhere close to using the full array of his skills, explaining,

> I think that, while we have value and we want to be productive—you know, I have certain skills and certain knowledge that, on the outside, people would pay me a lot of money to do. And it's not the money I'm thinking of, but you get certain value from your work. In here, you aren't allowed to do that. So how do we maintain our self-esteem by contributing to society? Because, you know, it's not just me. There's a lot of people in here that have a lot of skills that could be put to use, and we don't really have an outlet for them.

Many prisoners complain about the general lack of jobs and programs to keep them productively engaged. But this issue is magnified for lifers, who frequently are prevented from enrollment in programs, since the administration prioritizes those with release dates. If programs are meant to reduce recidivism, the thinking goes, then lifers should be denied entrance to them because they presumably will never be released.

Lifers understandably bemoan this reality. Not only do they chafe against the unwelcome idleness, but they also believe they can make programs better through their attendance.[18] Fred complained about this as he discussed his frustration at being left out of drug prevention classes. A three-striker whose offenses all stemmed from his drug habit, Fred thought he could be a valued contributor in any group drug-prevention program: "As an LWOP prisoner, they won't let me take substance abuse classes. They have these twelve- or eighteen-week classes. But they won't let any of the lifers take those classes. Which would be a real asset to those classes, you would think—if you had a guy doing a life sentence to go in there and talk about addiction and how that played a part getting him a life sentence." Gerald remarked, "You would think that they would give jobs to people who have life and keep them busy, because they have to stay here forever. But instead they don't; instead they treat you way different."

The paucity of challenging jobs generated numerous complaints from lifers. Older prisoners could recall a time when outside industries developed operations inside. These created well-paying, reasonably skilled jobs. But these were eliminated. The jobs that remained were lower skilled and less lucrative. And only a small percentage of those jobs could go to lifers. Said Sean,

> Idle time is a huge problem in prison. Now, I guess, basically everybody wants to be productive. I mean, even somebody who's lazy, they may not do the same things that someone else will do, but they want to feel like their life has value. You might have some people who are just looking to get out and are like: "Oh, I'll be out there in a year and a half, and I don't want to work, I don't want to do this." There are some of those, but for the majority—especially for people who have a long time to do—they want to feel productive.

Oscar, responding to a question about whether the loss of good jobs had any impact on the lives of prisoners, stated, "Yeah, it definitely has, in terms of what guys are able to buy and do and get around. The dearth of jobs for most people around here—the vast majority, probably 70 percent or more, don't have a job at all. Not even sweeping. It's miserable, if you want to have a life that's not just sitting around and doing nothing." From Melvin's perspective, good jobs enabled the development of a strong work ethic, something he saw lacking in many younger prisoners. If they hoped to ever avoid crime, they needed better work habits: "If you're gonna change, you've got to get up at six o'clock in the morning, go to that job, work for eight hours—a lot of these guys have never done that. And that's what guys need to be doing."

For Melvin himself, the desire was not just to stay productive: he had an additional wish to provide income for his family. His ability to be a breadwinner to some degree was important to his self-esteem. Describing a time when he had had a good job, he said, "I was happy because I was working, and I was able to help my family. That's a big thing for me, to be able to help my wife, do things for my son. To try to contribute to the family while not being there—that's huge."

Their desires to contribute thus led lifers to express considerable frustration with the dearth of opportunities to do so. That so many manage to still find constructive outlets for their energies illustrates again why their status as easy keepers is no small accomplishment. Another impediment that frustrates many lifers concerns their desire to find a satisfying means to atone for their crimes.

"YOU KNOW, IT'S REALLY ALL ABOUT PUNISHMENT": ON RETRIBUTION IN PRISON

As I noted in the introduction, the state of Washington, like many others in the United States, embraces retribution as its guiding philosophy of punishment. This philosophy maintains that criminals owe society a debt for their transgression. Criminals harm society and thus must provide recompense, usually in the form of time in prison. For Washington and other states, a corollary idea focuses on the equity of sentences. Because a given crime, say robbery, causes the same form of harm everywhere, then sentences for that crime should be uniform.

These philosophical precepts help legitimate so-called "fairness in sentencing" regimes. Such approaches mandate that sentences have a fixed length and that they be uniform. A particular harm demands a proportionate, consistent punishment. This differs from sentencing regimes that might emerge if rehabilitation were the guiding punishment policy. Then, you might wish sentences to be of indeterminate length. If this were the case, then prisoners' release dates could be tied to their behavior inside. This would give prisoners an incentive to engage in self-betterment.

Lifers consistently noted the downstream consequences of Washington's emphasis on retribution. The symbolic slights they described, the lack of adequate programming, and the scant and poorly paid jobs all gave lifers a pervasive sense that the only thing that mattered was that they were criminals who had to pay with their time. "It's really all about punishment; it's really all about retribution," Nate said. "Like, they're all mad at you. They're all here to punish you. And that is not productive, whatsoever."

Lifers had two issues with this state of affairs. One was the absence of a widespread spirit of rehabilitation in their prisons.[19] Aware of the personal and vocational deficits exhibited by younger prisoners with release dates, lifers fully expected to see those individuals back in prison after they were released. Burt, for example, remarked,

> The whole system is just more punishment-oriented. [The system is] not really working on rehabilitation in a real sense—[for example,] learning basic simple life skills. Like, maybe have all these guys, even if they're in for only a year and a day or whatever, take certain classes on basic life skills—parenting, basic financial responsibility, how to balance a checkbook, these kinds of things. We're pond scum in their view, and I'm not sure why. And not that

we should be mollycoddled by any means, but ... [we should] learn more, learn job skills—I'm talking about other guys more than myself—a chance to become whole more directly. I see some of these guys and the way they act. If they go out there and act that way, and if they've been down for a while, and they become negative and jaundiced and, I don't know, don't have a work ethic, they're going to come back. That's where recidivism happens.

William expressed a similar sentiment but took matters even further. He thought his prison should both provide more programs and create greater communication across prison staff. This way, each prisoner could be monitored and supported more closely. As he put it,

> We do a lot of punishing in prison. I would like for prisoners to actually be rehabilitated. Punishment shouldn't be a part of rehabilitation. So if I could actually change prison, I would like to see programs that actually deal with those who have been abused. Not just: "Okay, I'm gonna sign you up for a drug program," and you go down and some person teaches this drug program. I would like to see that person be responsible not only in the classroom but when he comes back to his unit. The officers should maintain a degree of observation, where they can say, "Hey, how John being?" You know, maybe John is doing pretty good in class, but John do not know how to interact with the people that he live with. And he's threatening people, and he's showing signs of violence, and he's been caught with a marijuana stick in his mouth. I would like to see this whole system involved in each person. That would be the change that I would make.

William also noted a second common complaint about the current practice of retribution. Central to the idea of retribution is that anyone who commits a criminal offense has damaged the social fabric and therefore has incurred a cost. Serving time in prison is one means by which such a cost can be paid. With enough time in prison, the criminal presumably pays back to society the debt created by the transgression. Atonement thus comes through incarceration. But lifers expressed considerable angst about this limited means to repair the damage they had caused. They wished for more numerous and potentially beneficial opportunities to repay the debt they felt they owed.

This desire to atone, as mentioned in chapter 1, motivated many prisoners to counsel others. Yet even those who engaged in such efforts believed that the reach of their influence was severely constricted if they remained imprisoned. Charlie, for example, knew exactly what he would do if he were released. His murders occurred when he was sixteen, so he was well acquainted with the experience of being a troubled teenager:

> I was telling my wife when my attorney mentioned it: "What would your plans be if you were to get out of prison?"[20] And my initial thought was: "Well, I don't even want to think about that right now, because I'm not going to get my hopes up and then just get them dashed." But I'd love to be able to give back. You know, I was a troubled kid. I'd love to give back to troubled kids, given the opportunity. There's countless ways you can give back, other than spending year after year in prison. Not only does it cost money, but at a certain point it's kind of purposeless, I think. There's so much you could do to show your utter remorse and the fact that you have changed.

For his part, William was frustrated that state policy prevented him from expressing his remorse directly to the victims of his crime of assault. He believed that he and his victims would heal more effectively if he could do so:

> I want to be able to go to them directly and tell them, "What I did was wrong. And I am very sorry for what I've done to you. Nobody deserves to be beat up, under no circumstances." And I would ask

them to forgive me. And I'd like to see good things happen in their lives. I know I can't do that, but that would be what I'd love to do. And I have gone to God with that and, from a religious standpoint of view, asked forgiveness for doing that to them. But I'd like to tell them personally and say I am so sorry. And as sentimental as I am, I'm sure I probably would shed a bunch of tears at the same time. So, morally, I would like to do that.

Whether William's wish should be granted is a legitimate question, but his unquenched desire to atone as directly as possible was a sentiment many lifers shared. My interviewees thus questioned a policy of retribution that simply generated a life sentence and left matters there. They saw no value in lives that often consisted of little more than enforced idleness and led inexorably to a lonely and shameful death.[21] Instead, they saw much benefit in ensuring that they could make strong and purposeful contributions. In this and other ways, they hoped that their lives could still be redeemed through their good works. They wished to atone in ways that seemed more directly related to the harms that they had caused. They wished, in effect, to earn some recognition for the work they do while playing the role of the easy keeper. They yearned for a means of repayment that could take a form other than the listless passage of time to an unredeemed death.

CONCLUSION: "IT'S GONNA BE ROADBLOCKS EVERYWHERE YOU GO"

Nate was among the more active lifers in his prison. He had a steady job, was active in several prisoner groups, and was an especially valued tutor in math classes. But he acknowledged the pervasive impediments that he daily confronted: "In every way, prison is a roadblock. But it's only as much of a roadblock as you let it be. It's definitely a stagnant environment. It's hard to move forward on things, but it's not impossible. So, as long as you keep that in your head, it's not impossible. But it's gonna be hard, it's gonna be roadblocks everywhere you go."

As I demonstrate in this chapter, life-sentenced prisoners must overcome considerable obstacles on their way to becoming an easy keeper. They must confront an ongoing stigmatization, a persistent limitation on their ability to forge steady personal relationships, and frequent restrictions on the jobs and activities they can pursue. Despite these challenges, many lifers still manage to construct lives of considerable purpose. They engage where they can in work and programs, they look for ways to support their peers inside and their loved ones on the outside. They pursue any available means to atone for their crimes. In short, they seek to write a redemptive script with their lives. That they do this in prison environments that are often stagnant and oppressive is a demonstration of their resilience, of their incessant yearning to be something other than a convict.

Yet life-sentenced prisoners will, like all of us, eventually age, decline, and ultimately die. This inescapable reality is a challenge for everyone but especially for prisoners, who live in environments not designed to care for the infirm. Thus, even as prisons clearly function better with easy keepers in their midst, so will they struggle to accommodate the inevitably complicated lives of the aged. Just as it is not easy for lifers to themselves be easy, so is it hard for prisons to grapple with the implications of so many declining prisoners.

CHAPTER THREE

When Easy Becomes Hard

Easy keepers improve the prisons that house them. They provide a calming influence on younger prisoners prone to disruption. They serve as role models. They seek to provide counsel to both staff and fellow prisoners to improve their communities.

Because of their standing, and because of many prisoners' reluctance to work too closely with prison staff, easy keepers often serve as the most significant resource for younger prisoners who seek to change and mature. As he talked about this type of work, Leonard was asked whether lifers were perhaps more influential than prison staff in helping the project of rehabilitation. He responded affirmatively:

> Oh, absolutely. People don't want to listen to the staff or the counselors. The counselors, they have such a huge caseload that it's hard for them to really focus on an individual. There's no way that you can really mentor somebody. You can say, "Well, I'm going to put you down for this program, this program, this program," and then people just wait and wait and wait. Months later, they're still waiting, because there's a waiting list on everything. In that sense, the

lifers have much better control over—they don't have control over who gets jobs and who doesn't get jobs. What they do have is the knowledge of how to get a job quicker and who to approach about jobs. How to go about it. How to write up a resume. Things like that in here, to help those guys. We have the upper hand because we live here. We know how the system works better than anybody that comes here that works eight hours a day. We live here twenty-four hours a day. In that sense, we know the underlying working of the facility much better than the staff that work here do.

Their knowledge, experience, and prestige thus allow easy keepers to play an indispensable role in their prison communities.

Yet no one remains easy forever. Life-sentenced prisoners inevitably age, decline, and die. In the process, they become significantly more difficult to house. As their numbers increase, so will the complications they create for prison systems. If less mobile, they will need assistance to get from place to place. If diseased, they will need increasing and often expensive medical attention. If cognitively impaired, they will require facilities that can assist them with their daily needs.

Because of these inevitable changes, institutions that house sizable numbers of life-sentenced prisoners will face considerable challenges. Even if easy keepers improve the institutions that house them—and in the process make life more manageable for prison staff—their eventual decline will create notable difficulties. As I will elaborate, prison staff struggle to meet the needs of elderly prisoners. Mobility is a key concern here. As prisoners lose the capacity to navigate stairs and inclines and to maneuver inside cramped cells, they become increasingly difficult to house. They also struggle to stay active. Finding jobs or programs for lifers is never a priority, and thus they cannot always stay engaged, even in the best of circumstances. And when their capacities erode, this challenge becomes magnified. Programs tailored to their specific needs are rare, and so elderly prisoners can sink into a listlessness that accomplishes little purpose, penological or otherwise. Finally, and unsurprisingly, lifers develop medical issues that can be complicated and costly. As I discuss below, prisons are already challenged to meet these medical realities effectively. This problem will only intensify as the large population of life-sentenced prisoners in the United States continues its inexorable path toward old age and death.

The significance of these realities emerged clearly in my conversations with prison staff. Of the twenty-seven staff with whom I spoke, eleven were classification counselors, ten medical professionals, and six custody staff members.[1] I selected these individuals because they are in a position to see the emerging challenges of a growing body of aging and declining prisoners. As the analysis below makes clear, these challenges are considerable and will only increase in the years ahead.

"IT JUST MAKES EVERYTHING MORE COMPLICATED": MOBILITY, ACCESSIBILITY, AND THE AGED PRISONER

Many American prisons were built with little attention to the needs of the mobility-impaired. This is certainly true of the Washington State Reformatory, which opened in 1910. It has four cell blocks, each of which contains four stories. To move from one part of the prison to another, each prisoner must get to the third floor of his cell block. The breezeway on that floor leads to another set of stairs, which prisoners must navigate to get to the dining area, to the yard, or to work or any other activity. Anyone without the capacity to manage these stairs will likely need to be transferred to another prison.[2] Mark, a classification counselor, described the situation: "As they get older, especially at the reformatory, we have problems because there's so many stairs. I mean, they even bother me. But, yeah, that's the first thing you start seeing, is that they have trouble getting up and down the stairs, trouble taking care of themselves because of getting up and down the stairs."

The Twin Rivers Unit is better in this regard. Prisoners there can live on the first floor of their units and can navigate the rest of the facility without encountering stairs. Yet it is still by no means easy to be mobility-impaired in prison. As Belinda, a health care professional, put it, "It makes it more challenging for everybody when they have some sort of physical ailment—if they have trouble ambulating or they're fragile in some way or have some sort of impairment or disability. It just makes everything more complicated." At Twin Rivers, even if an inmate can be allowed a wheelchair, he will likely still need to get into and out of his cell on his own. The cells are typically too small to allow a wheelchair inside. As Vern, a veteran custody staff officer, noted, "They won't be able to get [the wheelchair] in their cell, so they have to park the wheelchair out of their cell. Some people can get it in their cell; some guys can manage to get it in. We don't accept a lot of guys that are totally dependent on the wheelchair. We have guys that maybe can use a wheelchair, get up, and walk into their room. Our cells are not that big." So, even a facility that makes some accommodation for the mobility-impaired is necessarily limited to housing only some such prisoners. For that reason, Twin Rivers is seeking to expand the number of cells that comply with the Americans with Disabilities Act. Staff there indicate that the number of such cells must continue to increase.

Yet prison staff cannot handle the wheelchair-using population on their own. That is because the Twin Rivers campus is sloped. Thus, prisoners cannot get to meals, activities, visits, or medical attention without navigating hills. Those without adequate strength require a fellow prisoner to assist them. Because of this need, the prison pays some inmates to be "therapy aids."[3] Kevin, a counselor, noted the importance of these workers: "People that are confined to wheelchairs are not able to get back up the hills. So we assign them what we call a therapy aid, and their job is to get them wherever they need to go: medical visits, food, the inmate kitchen. That's their job, and they get paid for that, forty-two cents an hour. And some of them—I mean, that's better than nothing, it gets them a little store every month."[4]

The challenges of maintaining mobility are not the only ones facing many declining prisoners. Daily life inside a cell might itself pose problems. If assigned to a two-person cell, one of the individuals must be on a lower bunk. If a prisoner is cognitively impaired, he must have a cellmate who will not take advantage of him. If he has a particularly critical medical condition, such as cancer, he may require a cellmate who can monitor him closely. Tiffany, a counselor, explained,

> We have to be aware of it, so that we make sure they're housed in an appropriate cell. That's very, very important. We need to make sure that they're not at risk from a health standpoint. We need to make sure that their cellmate is compatible with them as well from a pre-risk standpoint, to make sure they wouldn't be victimizing somebody or be the victim of somebody. So that's very important. And then for custody staff to make sure that they have what they're supposed to have and that they don't have what they're not supposed to have.

It is a common challenge, according to prison staff, to make the necessary accommodations for many elderly prisoners. Part of the issue is the often-limited information staff may have about new prisoners sent to their institutions. Ideally, prison personnel are warned when they are about to receive someone who has special needs. But this is not always the case, according to Tiffany:

> If they come in off the chain, which is our transport from other facilities, and we didn't know in advance that they have a wheelchair—that information just didn't get communicated to whoever assigned the cell—we might have to then move them from one unit to a different unit that has a wheelchair-accessible cell. And I know from having been a unit sergeant [that] it can be difficult to manage when you have a lot of offenders who have what they call HSRs (which is health service request forms) for different medical exceptions. So they would have an HSR for a lower bunk, because they can't go to the upper bunk; and so we have to then assign them to a lower bunk. We have a lot of those. Some have HSRs for lower tiers, so then we have to make sure that their cell assignment is a lower bunk, lower tier. And the more we get of those, then we start to run out. That can pose a problem. And then sometimes we might have to, say, move them to a different wing or a different unit because there's none available here anymore—because we've kind of maxed out.

As Tiffany noted, the capacity of any given institution to accommodate an expanding range of health service requests will only lessen with time. With more easy keepers around, prisons' ability to meet their needs will steadily decline.

Medical conditions, of course, include cognitive impairments as well as physical ones. As challenging as it may be to find a place for a new prisoner whose mobility is limited, matters are arguably worse for those displaying signs of incipient dementia. Another counselor, Ulysses, described a situation that had arisen just before my conversation with him:

I had a guy recently who's an older prisoner. Got off the chain bus last week, and poses a problem because, well, we don't know where to put him. He should not, in my opinion, be in the general population, which he's not right now. He had to go back to the fourth-floor hospital here because he has used the bathroom on himself two or three times, and he doesn't care. So, the other offenders have to talk to him and get him to clean up, and this kind of stuff. He's just not mentally all there, and the general population facility would not be able to handle that. You have to get the paperwork to medical and mental health and get him seen, and you have to move him, and this kind of stuff. There are guys that are declining mentally or physically, and we have to deal with that.

Yet even if aging prisoners can be properly accommodated, they can still face difficulty integrating into the daily life of their institution. If they are impaired in any way, they often begin to isolate themselves, self-conscious as they are of their limitations and, perhaps, fearful of any of the more predatory prisoners. This tendency for isolation is compounded if their institution cannot make complete allowances for their limitations. Vern noted that older inmates may not fit into the general prison population.

If they're going to the mainline,[5] let's say they're older and they're well capable of walking, but they just don't fit in with a lot of groups. We have a couple of inmates who eat slower, so we have to give them a certain amount of time to eat. We have one inmate who we have to give at least more than the usual time, twenty minutes, to eat. More of them are on different diets. Recreation is totally different. Can a wheelchair guy go down into the gym? Yes, it's feasible, but can they do the same thing that a normal inmate can? Our recreation department is set up for normal guys, but we do modify it for those guys. We'll set up an eight o'clock period just for those guys to come in, and if they have any things to work on—

[instructions] from the doctor [that] say, "Hey, we need you to go in there and get your arms strengthened up or your legs strengthened up"—they can go in there and use the weight room. So we designate a certain time for those guys.

In short, neither of these Washington prisons is well equipped to address the many and varied complications that ensue as lifers age and decline. Even at Twin Rivers, where wheelchairs, walkers, and canes are allowed, prison staff still struggle to find the right unit, cell, cellmate, and bunk for each prisoner. As their diets become more specialized, as their self-consciousness about aging increases, as their cognitive and physical capacities become constricted, life-sentenced prisoners pose considerable challenges for the institutions that house them.

At some point, these complications become so extreme that prisoners must move to a facility better able to care for them. For those at the reformatory, that moment often comes when stairs become unnavigable. If their family is nearby, many in that situation will hope for a transfer to Twin Rivers. If they're already at Twin Rivers, the next destination might be a specialized minimum-security unit at the prison Coyote Ridge Corrections Center, in central Washington, which is designed along the lines of a nursing home. But prisoners typically resist being asked to move, and they have little say in where they are sent. So they rarely appreciate the demand that they move, and the move itself is typically complicated. John, another counselor, described this reality as it related to a prisoner who is almost eighty years old:

While he's still getting around pretty good, we are gonna have to start thinking about where we are gonna put him at some point. This guy might have been here for twenty-five years; all of his family lives in this area and now—where are we going to put him? We really try to take into consideration the contact these guys have with family members. We might say, "That guy has got to go to Coyote Ridge, because we don't have more bed space at Twin Rivers." Which is going to upset the family members: "Oh, this is my grandfather, and you're moving him all the way over there. He was doing so well." So you know those are hard conversations that we have to have sometimes.

Another counselor, Angela, made much the same point, but indicated that moves can be time-consuming and disruptive for staff as well:

Generally, once they're settled in, and they get kind of moved in, they don't want to pack up and move all their stuff. It can be very inconvenient. Also it's a lot of work for staff because they have to generate a move sheet that has to go to main control; and main control has to update their count sheet on the computer and their picture cards. The unit has to update their picture cards and their count, and then that has to get sent to records, and that has to update in our OMNI system, which is our Offender Management Networking Information System. So, there's a lot of work that goes into every single offender move that people don't really realize—all the time that it takes, and that it affects a lot of different areas.

As I discuss in more depth in chapter 4, there are few facilities in Washington that can attend to the needs of frail prisoners. The special needs unit at Coyote Ridge, called the Sage Unit, is a minimum-security facility. Few prisoners with a life sentence can live there. A minimum-security unit is less securely constructed and less intensively controlled than other prisons.[6] Because of their sentences, lifers are can rarely be assigned to minimum-security units even if they are infirm. Absent an infrequently granted exemption, lifers whose cognitive impairments impede their capacity for self care can be sent to either a prison hospital or a prison dedicated to those with mental health issues.

For the time being, then, prisons like the Washington State Reformatory and the Twin Rivers Unit house individuals with extensive needs. Many of these needs are already proving hard to meet. This includes aging prisoners' need to stay physically and mentally active.

"I JUST TALK ABOUT NONSENSE": KEEPING AN EASY KEEPER BUSY

Odell, a veteran staff member at the Washington State Reformatory, had, like many classification counselors, previously worked on the custody staff. In both of these roles, he had regular contact with life-sentenced prisoners. He appreciated the role they played in the prison where he worked, but he recognized the difficulties they faced in staying engaged. He even expressed some reluctance to talk with me, knowing as he did that many lifers cannot do much in his prison. His goal as a counselor is to get all the prisoners he works with engaged in meaningful activity. Over the course of our conversation, his frustration at his inability to do more to help lifers became evident:

> We want them to program. And, say they don't, we want to hold them accountable. But you kind of can't, because there's not a whole lot we can do for them. Or some of those guys can't be going out to the activities building, where education is, and some of the programs are held out there, and different classes that are offered. And then, that's where the library is, too, so they can't go out there to get library books; they can't read library books. A lot of times they are just out of sight, out of mind; and they are on a list, trying to get in programming, but it's no fault of their own [that] they don't have anything. So like I said, it's difficult to manage because, well, he's seventy and he's done all the programming that was asked of him. I mean he's done everything. There's nothing else for him to do. So

they just keep busy by just doing life. Talking to their friends, reading books, doing letters, communicating through email, working if they are lucky to have a job. Like I said, I was stumped. I almost didn't want to do the interview, because I was like: "I have nothing. I just talk about nonsense."

Easy keepers thus can struggle to stay active. Part of the issue is the prison system's preference for allocating spots in programs to individuals with release dates. As noted earlier, if any program is designed to reduce recidivism, then prison officials argue that it is wasted on individuals who will never be released. Lifers are also frequently passed over when jobs and other opportunities are made available. When asked about the biggest challenge he faces in working with lifers, Bill, a counselor, raised this issue:

The biggest challenge I see is the goal of DOC. Rehabilitation doesn't prioritize lifers. It focuses on guys with high needs—for drugs and alcohol, aggression, sexual deviancy. There's programs that are made for those kind of guys. But the lifers are never prioritized for those programs. You let them sit, and their needs aren't being addressed. They're still susceptible to the same behavior, criminal behavior, because they haven't taken anything that would address that. They also aren't prioritized for jobs. We have job availability, and a short-term person with five years may get clearance to work the job that has dangerous tools faster than a lifer [would]. A lot of times, lifers will be frustrated, because they have no infraction history or they haven't got an infraction in five years. But someone is here who's only been here for three years—he's been in a fight, he has a negative behavior pattern, and he still gets to do things that they don't. They feel it's a double standard. So then that creates resistance when you try to talk to them as a counselor, [when] you try to get them into programming, because they see that as: "You're just trying to get me to do something so it can pop up on my computer file. You're not doing it for me. DOC only wants me to program when it's convenient for them." That's how they look at it.

Jobs in prison are hard to come by, for anyone. Even though they pay meagerly, jobs are desired by prisoners looking for some form of constructive activity and the means to buy extra food, toiletries, or other items from the commissary. Easy keepers almost always seek work, given their desires for a routinized and positive existence. Yet jobs are hard to win and can easily be lost. Larry, a counselor, addressed this reality:

> There was one guy that just lost his job recently for horseplay. One guy came up and pushed him, and he pushed him back; and it almost turned into a fight. But he ended up losing his job. So now— he's an LWOP—he's mad because he lost his job. He has to wait to get hired again, and that was a big part of his routine. You work all day, get off work, shower, use the phone—there was a good routine that he had going. Now he doesn't have a job, and he loses money, so he can't buy items off the store like he normally does. Doesn't have a whole lot of family that sends him anything, so he was pretty much self-sufficient. Now he goes to the bottom of the list, and he has to work his way up, which makes it difficult.

A decreased physical capacity can further compound lifers' struggle to find employment. Most prison jobs require manual labor, which can pose a challenge for easy keepers whose abilities are waning with age. Angela recognized this as a significant reality for many:

> I had another one who was seventy-eight, and he wants to work. He wants to work, he's eligible to work, but he's frail. Where do you put him? Maintenance had an opening, but it's like: you've got to push this hundred-something-pound cart around with tools in it. He wasn't physically capable to do the job. So where do you put him? A lot of the jobs require physical work. They are mandated by policy to do programming whether it's school or work, some form of education or work. Sometimes you get creative! Sometimes it's like: Can they sweep the floor on the unit? What can they do? But then,

they feel demeaned, because they want to work, and it's like: you don't want to demean them, but you want to keep them busy.

For prisoners on dialysis, their treatment is the sum total of their "programming." They require treatment three days a week. Their other days are largely devoted to recovering from the treatment.

Cognitive impairments can be just as debilitating as physical ones for prisoners who want to work. Larry's caseload included prisoners who exemplified this challenge:

> I had one that was on my caseload that—it was hitting him really quick, and it was really concerning. His supervisor actually contacted me: "We have a problem. He doesn't know where he is." So, it was getting people involved: Do we need tests? Is there medication? Do we need to look at a different job? We had one guy that had dementia, and he really didn't know where he was. He would wander off, literally, because he was working in the kitchen just wiping tables to keep him occupied; they wouldn't accept him. So now we have a vulnerable elderly man in a general population environment who half the time doesn't know where he is. We have to lead him back. He will wander off down the hallway.

Given that their impairments can steadily accumulate, lifers would clearly benefit from programming specifically oriented to them. But such programs are a striking rarity. Angela was particularly forceful in noting this lack:

> ANGELA: We also have an aging population, but we don't have any type of adult-living-skills classes. How do you maintain mobility? I mean, you look at the general population, you look outside prison: we have aging [populations]. Look at a nursing home: they have mobility classes. How do you function? How do you get out of bed? How do you maintain a sore back? How do you do this? We don't teach them this, which ages them

even quicker. So you're sleeping on a mattress on a steel plate for twenty-something years. It's going to mess you up. How do you exercise? How do you maintain that physical mobility to be healthy, to curb some of that? We don't have an exercise program for an aging population. They can't get out there and run laps. Some of them can hardly get out there and walk the lap. Maybe their mobility is not good enough, so how can they do things tailored to a geriatric population?

HERBERT: There's nothing tailored to them at all?

ANGELA: Nothing.

HERBERT: Period?

ANGELA: Period. Nothing.

Unsurprisingly, staff possess concerns about aging prisoners whose abilities decline, given the dearth of activities in which they can engage.[7] The possibility of self-isolation emerges strongly. Sam, a veteran custody officer, recognized such individuals on his unit and did what he could to engage them. He could see the steady deterioration of their abilities and how their increased withdrawal fed depression, which then made engagement yet more difficult. He was asked what he did in such situations:

SAM: Just really monitor them ..., just keep an eye on them. Because their whole world now is their cell. Say they have a TV in there; maybe they have visits, maybe they don't. So these are the ones you just kind of have to keep an eye on. But we have so many offenders, it's hard. Some stand out more than others, but at some point [for] those guys that becomes their world: it's just their cell.

HERBERT: Just watch TV all day or ...?

SAM: Watch TV all day. ... I mean they're limited—their activities—as they get older, and that makes it hard. I think it's hard for them because they've done thirty to forty years, they're in their seventies, they can't go to rec like they used to, or they can't get around really well. Now, their whole world has become their cell. Those guys, we need to try to encourage to be more active.

As much, then, as typical easy keepers yearn for jobs and other opportunities to be constructively active, their inevitable physical and cognitive decline imperils this quest. This is especially true in prison environments that have little capacity to attend to their special needs. As Odell said, "There's not a whole lot that you can try and tailor to them. There's not a whole lot of opportunities."

Easy keepers can become much harder to maintain in prison environments ill-equipped to handle them. This reality is all the more apparent when one recognizes the very significant challenges prisons face in attending to the growing medical needs that aging prisoners will increasingly generate.

"VERY DRAINING POPULATION HERE": THE CHALLENGES OF HEALTH CARE

Greg was a prison doctor, a position he took after retiring as a private family physician. He took the job out of a desire to be of service to a population that he knew needed quality care. He enjoyed the work and the myriad challenges that he confronted daily. No day was like any other, he said. Indeed, no day ever went as he planned: "I'd say I've never had a day go as I wanted it to go, just in terms of planning. You have to be very flexible; you have to be very patient."

What made the work especially daunting, he said, was the nature of the prisoner population. Their needs were many, their general health was commonly poor, and the conditions for providing and maintaining care were often suboptimal. "Very draining population here," Greg said. "These are the guys you weeded out of your practice when you were in private practice, and here you're stuck with them. You can't weed them out." Because most prisoners are from impoverished backgrounds, many of them did not encounter quality health care before their incarceration. Further, many of them abused alcohol or drugs and, thus, placed considerable additional strain on their physical health.[8] Given this background, and given the sheer size of the prisoner population, it is no surprise that prison health care providers frequently tell stories about a wide range of serious health problems that they struggle to address.[9] Greg commented, "Most prisoners are ahead of their chronologic age, with their physiological age. Their bodies look twenty years older than they are. That has a lot to do with how they took care of themselves early on."

Health care providers who come to work in prison after time in outside clinics or hospitals describe a sense of surprise at the number of complicated cases that they see among the inmates. Edward, a longtime prison nurse, explained,

A lot of these guys have not had very good care on the outside, so we've seen some really rare forms of cancer. Even our doctor, who's been a doctor for forty years, will every once in a while be caught: "I have never seen this in my entire practice." So, very complex cases. We have a lot of cancer guys—lung cancer, we get bowel cancer, we've had a rash of guys who've had some brain cancer issues—you name it. And so we work with the specialists, and we have some guys that go out on a weekly basis for chemotherapy treatment. One particular guy goes out, and we have a whole packet of stuff we send with him to the cancer care clinic. They get him set up with the chemo, then he is still on the chemo infusion through a pump. He goes over to the prison hospital until the infusion's complete and then he comes back here, back to his outpatient setting, until the next round. We have to do blood-test monitoring to make sure that he's tolerating the treatment, because sometimes, if it's wiping out, say, the white blood cells or something like that, then he is not at a point where he can receive the next dosing. Sometimes we have to cancel trips, depending on what the lab work is showing. So there's a lot of complexities in managing these guys.

Fiona, another nurse, described a similar reality:

> We have a lot of diabetics, as many as thirty, thirty-five, sometimes, who are coming to diabetic lineup three or four times a day. We have a lot of cancer guys who go out on a regular basis for chemotherapy or follow-ups, or various things like that. We have some guys who are on IV medications to control bowel issues. We have many guys who are on a blood thinner because of maybe a history of stroke or heart valve issues, heart rhythm issues, things like that. So we have to do ongoing finger strips to monitor, to make sure the particular medication is not making the blood too thin, or we're keeping within therapeutic levels so they're not at risk for developing a clot. We have a lot of those guys that we see on a regular basis.

Other health care providers described complications in prisoners who have suffered gunshot wounds in the past, and whose bodies are thereby compromised. Others mentioned how histories of drug abuse can increase levels of tolerance for pain medications. As a result of this, prison doctors struggle to provide relief from pain without creating or exacerbating an addiction problem. Said Ike, a prison doctor, "We are trying to treat these chronic pain patients in a more effective way. I will say that we plan, we do, but we haven't really come up with anything."

Because of their sheer numbers and the range of preexisting conditions they harbor, prisoners pose pressing challenges to medical staff, particularly as the aging process advances. Structural issues in the prison can further exacerbate the challenges of providing quality health care.

Part of the issue is diet. As one health care professional put it, "It's carbs and carbs and carbs. Sugar, carbs, sodium. It's all carbs and sodium." A nurse made a similar complaint, particularly about the food available from the prison commissary: "If you look at what's on the store, 75 percent of it is junk food. Sugar, chips, and stuff like that."

Prison health care providers also complain about the reality of prisoners living in such close quarters. Because of this unavoidable reality, stemming the spread of contagious diseases is close to impossible. Said one nurse, "You get the flu here, and you've got yourself a real doozy."

Staff encounter a range of other obstacles to the provision of effective treatment. A key issue for many staff is the simple challenge of hiring and retaining high-quality health care professionals. Prison facilities typically pay less than outside providers and require working with a stigmatized population. Because of the continual staff shortage, health care providers often work overtime simply to meet the basic medical needs of the population. That makes more attentive and overarching care elusive. Fiona addressed this issue while noting the lack of case management services that she would like to see the prison provide:

> We need a full staff, just because of the time it takes to take care of all of them. It's that case management and coordinating everything—these guys are needing to provide them adequate health care. That's one of the biggest challenges. Overseeing and making sure that after they've gone out, say, on an outside trip, and the specialist is recommending follow-up treatment, that we make sure that we're following up and looking at that and getting the approvals that we need to do what we need to do.

Even when staff are operating at close to capacity, their ability to provide care is troubled by the sheer volume of the work and by frequent interruptions. One example of the workload is the "pill line" for individuals who need medication for diabetes. It commonly forms four times a day at Twin Rivers Unit, and the line is so long that it can take up to one hour to receive medication. This diabetes-focused pill allocation does not, of course, include the myriad other medications that many prisoners take daily.

Among the interruptions, a common one involves inmates suffering from seizures or some other form of medical emergency. One such situation arose during my interview with Fiona. As we were talking, an urgent message came over the nearby radio.

> FIONA: The nurses will respond to that. They're responding to a medical emergency right now. So that means they shut down the clinic, they respond—two nurses will respond with a medical gurney and an officer to the scene to assess [it]. And they usually then bring the guy back here to monitor and have the provider see the person.
>
> HERBERT: Do you need to go?
>
> FIONA: No, there are two nurses out there that can respond.
>
> HERBERT: So, this sort of things happens ...?
>
> FIONA: Regularly. Regularly.
>
> HERBERT: Multiple times a week?
>
> FIONA: Multiple times a day.

Vern, who is commonly responsible for overseeing the group that responds to medical emergencies, noted both the increased frequency of such events and the disruptive impact they have on the institution. If his unit must respond to an emergency, the entire prison is put on hold until the situation is cleared: "So when I say *secure,* when we're dealing with that situation, nothing moves. Inmates stay locked in their area until we secure the area: they're locked in their rooms—they can't come out of their rooms, no activities can be done, all officers are on alert. Even in outer areas, no inmates should be coming and moving when we are dealing with that situation." Vern indicated that such emergency actions were becoming more common as the number of aging prisoners increased. The disruptions to prison life, including the provision of regular health care, were more frequent as a consequence of a larger population of elderly inmates.

The provision of good-quality and comprehensive care is further compromised by the basic terms on which prison health care is provided. The health plan that governs prison medical care is not exactly expansive. Greg explained the situation to me:

GREG: On the outside, your customers are your patients. Inside prison, your customer is the public. It's a trust that John Q. Public puts on us to spend money wisely. We have the Offender Health Plan, which says we've committed ourselves to preservation of life or limb, and beyond that everything is negotiable. Like, we don't fix ACL [anterior cruciate ligament] tears. A young guy who's twenty-five years old rips his ACL playing basketball down here and has got another twenty years to go in prison—that's a big deal to them. I think we ought to fix it, but we don't. It costs a lot of money to fix them. So the Offender Health Plan really defines the standard of care within prison. It's a much different standard of care than on the outside.

HERBERT: How would you characterize the difference?

GREG: Just that we're committed to preservation of life or limb, and beyond that everything is negotiable. So a lot of dermatology we don't treat. If you came in with a bunch of moles that you said you want off, I'd take them off. But if they look benign in here, we don't take them off; we don't treat them. We try to shift a lot of the responsibility to the patient, especially when the issue comes to chronic pain.

Although prisoner complaints were impossible to verify, many inmates suggested that the ability of the prison to meet their medical needs regularly fell short of the mark. Dean, a lifer, used a particularly elaborate example to explain this:

> It's a hard job for them here to provide high-quality health care, because there's so many people here that are getting older in prison and are requiring more and more care. They have to cut and make sacrifices in other areas to help them with the cost of the medication that people are taking for different reasons. I don't think it's very good. For example, there's a lot of guys in the facility right now that have hernias. They're bulging out and everything. They won't fix them, because they say it's not life-threatening. Now they're at the point of—if it's not a life-threatening kind of an injury, they're not going to fix it. People pay for it yourself. They have medical accounts here where you can have money sent in or whatever. Or if your insurance covers it, then you can have the stuff done. But they don't pay for it hardly ever. Unless there's an underlying reason that they have to. Life-threatening or something like that. A friend of mine walked around for two weeks with a broken collarbone. He went up there and they x-rayed, and it was broken. They wouldn't fix it for two weeks. Finally he kept complaining. "Hey, I can't even lift my arm. It's getting worse." You know, it's getting all black and blue. It's just horrible, right? Two weeks later they took him in and got it fixed, but he had to really fight to get them to do that. They said it wasn't life-threatening. It's not the best; it really isn't.

Sean had a similar complaint, about the long-standing pain that emanated from a medical condition that proved resistant to diagnosis:

> The biggest problem that I have—the problem that I think could be alleviated—is sleep. I can't sleep worth a darn, because I have so much pain—back pain—and I go numb. I don't really think that I can get a therapeutic mattress, which I think they have.

Unfortunately, there is a very rigid set of rules for who gets that, because they don't want everyone to say that they need it. But there is probably a rigid set of rules because of people with bedsores or documented back surgery. And my situation is very unique because I don't know what I have; and so, because of that, I'm not going to fit into any category. I've done all I can, but I don't necessarily know the best way to do it.

Because of the limitations of the health care plan provided to prisoners, many medical issues are either untreated or referred to a statewide committee for consideration. This committee, which meets weekly, includes medical staff from a number of prison facilities. Edward notes that these tough-to-call cases lead to some difficult decisions. He used the example of an aging inmate whose arthritis had reduced his mobility:

> At what point are decisions made? This prisoner has arthritic changes in their body. Is that hip replacement, or is that shoulder replacement, really medically necessary? There's ethical pieces in there that you have to look at. What is the impact on the entire facility when this patient has a bad hip, a really severe hip? We could say that, already, that's taxpayers' money to replace that hip. But then you look at: if he can't be mobile, then he's going to have to be in a walker or be in a wheelchair, so that's going to take more care. If we fix it . . .
>
> I see those kinds of issues, and we have had some really interesting ethical conversations.

The need for such conversations will obviously only increase as the life-sentenced population becomes more arthritic and beset by the other common ailments that accompany aging. The need will also grow for prisoners to be taken outside in search of the more complex medical care that a prison clinic or hospital cannot provide.

Paul, a lieutenant, was well aware of this challenge. His principal responsibility was to coordinate the fleet of vehicles and accompanying staff needed to get prisoners to various medical appointments in the region. He described his job as a "logistical nightmare" and one that required him to regularly force his staff to work overtime. He described a common reality with which his staff must cope: a trip to a Seattle hospital with a cancer-stricken inmate:

PAUL: Those trips at times take up to twelve hours. Not to include my drive time.

HERBERT: Twelve hours at the facility?

PAUL: Yes. Once they get there, they have pre-procedure blood draws that they have to do. Then they go in to get their treatment, and it takes six to eight hours to receive all of their treatment. And then they have to wait two hours and get another blood draw to see what their platelet counts are at. So some of those trips are pretty lengthy.

HERBERT: And you have two guys there the whole time?

PAUL: Sitting there with them. And unless they are admitted to a room, my transport team has to stay there with them. Once they're admitted, it turns into a hospital watch. One officer can stay with them; my transport team can come back and do other trips.

HERBERT: Sounds like, logistically, it must be challenging.

PAUL: Oh, it's a nightmare *[laughs]*.

The fact that many health care facilities will see prisoners only during limited hours makes this coordination especially difficult. As Paul indicated, "We're kind of at their mercy, because they don't have to accept that offender as a patient." Some providers, he indicated, were afraid of complaints from the public or were leery of attempting to coordinate care with overworked prison staff. Given these various constraints, and the increasing need for medical attention for aging prisoners, Paul estimated his staff would accumulate as much as $250,000 in overtime compensation during any given year.

Perhaps the most challenging medical situation for prison staff is when inmates begin to display signs of dementia. All of the prison medical staff who mentioned dementia described the same dilemma entailed in trying to provide good-quality humane care.[10] This is an especially acute problem for individuals with life sentences, who, as noted above, are not likely to be considered admissible to the only prison unit in Washington built to assist inmates who cannot complete their ordinary daily activities. At the Monroe Correctional Complex, such individuals often go to the hospital at the reformatory, located on the fourth floor. Carly, a nurse, was particularly direct in describing the challenge:

> CARLY: We're not equipped anywhere in general population to deal with dementia. Across the board, we are not equipped to deal with that.
> HERBERT: Can you really deal with it on the fourth floor, either?
> CARLY: We can, because it's what we have to do.

Edward made a similar point when describing how they approached an inmate with dementia who lived in the prison hospital for several months: "What do you do? We modified things the best that we could, and he took a lot of time. And a lot of nursing care, because he would be incontinent of stool—numerous times in the day—just a lot of heavy care. So you had to make allowances. And make it work. What do you do? You have to."

In the following exchange, Edward perhaps betrayed the struggle they face in finding an appropriate place for such an individual.

EDWARD: Some are really not that physically compromised, but there are some that have dementia. So, where does that person go?

HERBERT: Where does that person go?

EDWARD: Exactly.

HERBERT: I mean, right now, where does he go?

EDWARD: Well, now we'll hide—we'll house them up in the inpatient unit.

The inpatient hospital is the location for another increasingly common phenomenon—a prisoner's death. When an approaching death leaves life-sentenced prisoners too frail to be in the general population, they typically are sent to the fourth floor. This is not a place where prisoners commonly wish to be. As Carly notes, "They absolutely hate it, because they're cut off from their social circle, from just going to mainline. I think that adds to this long-term issue, because it's depressing."

As Carly further notes, the hospital staff do all that they can to make a dying prisoner's last days as comfortable as possible.[11] They provide soft foods, they allow fellow inmates and visitors to come to the fourth floor to say their good-byes, and they provide as much individual attention as they can. Staff will also work to keep a dying inmate housed at Monroe if they know his family is nearby. In that way, the staff seek to keep the dying prisoner as comfortable and secure as possible. But these measures cannot discount the fact that an inmate is dying in prison. "Even though someone is sick or dying, they live in a cell. That's what the rooms on the fourth floor are. They're cells," Carly explained. "Some of the things we would do for people at hospice at home—like massive amounts of meds, because there's always somebody right there with them—it doesn't work so great in our system."[12]

In myriad ways, then, the large and growing population of aging prisoners generated by the surge in life sentences creates significant complications for prison medical personnel, who are understaffed and underresourced. They seek to balance a restricted health care plan against emerging medical needs; they engage in regular ethical debates about just how much care to provide; they encounter disruptions from the increased number of medical emergencies; and they struggle to provide humane care to those who suffer from dementia and those approaching death. Ike's description of how his staff respond to the general challenge of dealing with those with dementia—"We improvise all the time"— is perhaps a fair assessment of the general reality for prison medical staff forced to meet the needs of an aging population. The skill of their improvisations should not be discounted, but neither should the structural impediments that confront them, ones that will only grow more severe as lifers steadily accumulate in America's prisons.

CONCLUSION: "WILL IT WORK? I DON'T KNOW"

Like Leonard, Melvin believed his work in counseling younger prisoners was likely more effective than that offered by prison staff. He attributed this largely to the common prison norm of resisting prison staff. As he put it,

> Nobody wants to listen to DOC. They don't. And so when they see guys like me that's done twenty-five years and still out there doin' stuff, and knowing how bad that I wanna go home with my family—because everybody knows about my family; they probably listen to more than they want to. But I love my family. And I tell them, "There's nothing more important than your family." I tell them, "You've got a mom. I've lost mine since I've been in prison." And

you see things in their face—they've never thought about that. [They] never think about being in prison so long that they lose their moms in prison. Those are the things that I try to put in their head to maybe think about it a little bit. Will it work? I don't know.

Melvin is rightly skeptical about his ability to effect change in other people. It is always a difficult task. But his question applies just as well to America's practice of subjecting a growing number of people to life sentences. Even if Melvin, like many other easy keepers, works to make the daily operations of his prison more smooth, his inevitable decline will complicate his daily life. Thus, just as Melvin struggles with the reality of his sentence, so will his prison struggle to meet his needs. As prison staff make clear, these needs are numerous, complicated, and costly. Even if life sentences prevent individuals from committing crime on the outside, they cannot slow the inexorable processes of aging and death. In the long run, then, American prison staffs will struggle to accommodate life-sentenced inmates whose needs will multiply considerably in the years ahead.

In short, it is impossible for easy keepers to be easy forever. Because of this, perhaps it is time to reconsider the policies that generate life sentences, and to otherwise recast the futures of those who currently have been permanently banished behind bars. Perhaps it is time for the rest of us to ease up.

CHAPTER FOUR

Let's All Be Easy

At the time of our first conversation, Edgar was a life-sentenced prisoner, one who earned his punishment via Washington's "three strikes and you're out" law. Then fifty-three, Edgar had spent much of his adult life in prison while living an existence he called largely meaningless.

That reality had changed about five years earlier, when Edgar began to devote himself to art. Entirely self-taught, he spent countless hours in his cell crafting pen-and-ink drawings of notable intricacy. His self-confidence developed along with his skill: "I didn't like myself until I started drawing and doing what I was doing. That, being able to create, is big for me. Because I get rid of a lot of stuff that I don't want, or stuff that is in me I can beautify and make it better. I can take stuff that's in my head and get rid of it. And *[laughs]* it works." Beyond devoting himself to his craft, Edgar tried to inspire others. He occasionally taught art classes to his fellow prisoners, something he found gratifying:

EDGAR: It's kind of hard to lasso them in, because they're into video games and all that. If you can get someone that's into video games and music and all that, and pull them over so they slow down and concentrate on doing some drawing, it just pulls a whole other person out of there; just a whole other person shows up.

HERBERT: That's interesting.

EDGAR: Yeah, and I enjoy it. It makes me feel good.

HERBERT: To help people do that?

EDGAR: Oh, yeah, to help them and to see it blossom. I mean, it's great.

Despite the benefits he derived from creating and teaching art, Edgar still expressed considerable frustration. In his experience, the prison restricted his creative reach by limiting the size of his works. As he put it,

[My art] is a passion. I know I'm good at it. I know I look at things differently. I know I have the ability to do it, and I'm excited about it. Now, what's happened [is], you can only buy paper that's so big, per policy. So our canvases are only so big: we can't get no big things like that. So now, I want to expand, I want to go larger because I'm ready to. And I can't. *[Laughs]* See what I'm saying? It's a visual thing and it's defeating, but now it's the prize. I gotta keep my hope up and stay positive and keep going, because there's things that I want to do and paint that I won't do on the smaller scale, because they deserve a larger stage. They deserve a bigger canvas, to be able to bring out what I want to do.

"I DIDN'T WANT ONE MOMENT IN MY LIFE TO DEFINE ME": RECONSIDERING THE EASY KEEPER

Edgar's need for a bigger canvas, metaphorically speaking, is shared by many other easy keepers. He is hardly alone in his desire to find more ample and fulfilling opportunities to engage in productive activities. Despite his oppressive sentence, Edgar still sought to find a means to realize his human potential, to rescue a creative impulse from a life of possibly overwhelming despair.

The resilience and creativity of easy keepers like Edgar are rarely considered when punishment policy is debated and enacted. The previous chapters demonstrate the detriment of such neglect. Easy keepers are as numerous in America's prisons as they are productive forces. Both prisoners and staff acknowledge that easy keepers provide a source of stability and leadership that enables institutions to run more smoothly. They mentor and calm younger prisoners prone to disruption, they establish routines for others to model, they engage constructively with staff to resolve tensions. They search relentlessly for productive outlets for their energies. They demonstrate a stunning degree of resiliency. They retain hope when anguish could easily overcome them.

These accomplishments deserve recognition in three areas in particular. First, prisons should provide more ample and satisfying outlets for the fecund energies of easy keepers. As constructive as many easy keepers may be, many still long for yet more opportunities to enhance both themselves and their communities. Social dynamics both inside and outside America's prisons would benefit if easy keepers had manifold chances to develop and share their various capacities.

Second, prison staff should continually question the balance they strike between custody and care. On the one hand, prisons simply must maintain high levels of security. The first priority of custody staff is to ensure that everyone inside is as safe as possible. Threats to bodily security must be both anticipated before they can occur and responded to effectively when they do. For that reason, it is understandable that prison staff so assiduously maintain routines to maximize safety and security. On the other hand, slavish devotion to such routines can inhibit humane treatment, particularly for individuals who are aging and declining. If America's prisons are forced to house a growing population of aging inmates—and if policy changes do not occur, that is precisely what will happen—then they must begin to consider how to make those inmates comfortable as their bodies begin to fail. This will require an ongoing willingness to consider changes to the security regimes that characterize prisons.

Of course, one of the means to minimize the difficulties of managing an aging prisoner population is to change punishment policy, the third focus of this chapter. If easy keepers so amply demonstrate maturity and thoroughgoing altruism, then they deserve greater opportunities for release. Like many other states, Washington disallowed parole in the mid-1980s, and thus most life-sentenced prisoners there will never be released, absent a change in law.[1] Given that easy keepers no longer pose a public safety threat, their continued incarceration is hard to justify.[2] This is particularly true because of the severe consequences that will befall prison systems unprepared for the aging population that is steadily growing in their midst. Unless America wishes for a raft of prisons crafted like nursing homes, policy changes must transpire.

The need for reconsidering punishment policy derives, at root, from the need to recognize who easy keepers become. Their projects of self-actualization and their desires for redemption deserve acknowledgment. Here, it is worth bearing in mind the words of Charlie, who poignantly explained why he became motivated to complete his projects of self-betterment:

I didn't want one moment in my life to define me. I didn't want my crime to define the person that I was. DOC has so many labels and so many restrictions on guys with life without, that I came to the understanding with myself that I wasn't going to let that define who I became. I was going to do all I could with what I had, and I was going to become a better person. I still might never ever get out. Chances are I won't, but I'm not going to let that be an excuse to be an idiot, a delinquent that just wreaks havoc. This doesn't come from anything the DOC has done or tried to do to get me to change. This is coming from me as a person, growing as a person, growing up as a person from the kid who didn't even have any idea of what he was doing.

Charlie's growth is neither an accident nor an anomaly. To consider carefully the efforts that he and other easy keepers daily exert is to take an important step toward reforming American punishment in ways that would benefit all of us.

"THAT'S THE ONLY TIME I EVER FELT I COULD BE MORE THAN I AM": HONORING AND DEVELOPING THE HUMAN CAPITAL OF LIFE-SENTENCED PRISONERS

Rudy received his life-without-parole sentence as a teenager. His journey through prison was a common one. Scared and vulnerable, he felt compelled to join an ethnically defined gang. The persistent violence that ensued led to several trips to solitary confinement. Maturity eventually set in, and he modified his ways. His better behavior made him a candidate for a novel program in a prison where he previously lived: he was allowed to become a dog trainer. He described, with enthusiasm, what his first day with a dog felt like:

The first time I ever had a dog in the cell it just kind of tripped me out. It's like, "There's a dog in the cell!" When they brought this little dog the first time—this little dachshund, whatever they call them, it's one of the small little dogs; it looks like a wiener dog—anyway, they bring it in here, and it immediately just walks right in and sits next to me, and it was the coolest thing I've ever seen. That really kept me out of trouble, because if you got a major infraction you could get kicked out of the program. That really did something for me.

As Rudy explained it, the dog program promoted a heightened sense of responsibility:

I was sitting there taking care of another living thing. It just really gave me a little more peace than normal, because I felt it was a good responsibility. It was just amazing, at a whole other level, especially taking care of another creature. It's something that can look at you and be dependent on you. It's a whole, entirely different level. It was both exciting, it was liberating, and maturing. It gave me responsibility. I had to take care of this thing, but I had to keep myself out of trouble and stay away from people who were causing trouble.

Later in the interview, Rudy again returned to the significance of his work as a dog trainer: "The only time I've ever been part of something was during the dog program. That was something that gave me a reason to be something more than I am, because I was given a big responsibility to be something. That's the only time I ever felt in my life I ever had to be more than I am. The only time in my life. That's the only time I ever felt I could be more than I am, because I had to take care of something that I had great responsibility over."

Rudy's enthusiasm for his work as a dog trainer is compelling, but so is his implicit complaint that no other such opportunities are available to him. Lifers are well aware of their scorned status and grow reluctantly accustomed to being forced to the end of the line. Charlie captured this sense of resignation well:

When you're a lifer, every time you go for a hearing, or anytime you go for anything, they always have your file. And on your file [is] a big stamp that has "LWOP," life without parole; so they automatically perceive you as someone different than someone who is just on their way out or, you know. It definitely plays a part in where you can get transferred to, how high you can go up on the custody level, things like that. Certain instances, it bars you from getting into programs that are more geared to people that are getting out. So it seems like we're always at the back of the bus.

Easy keepers, unsurprisingly, chafe under this status. They see themselves as eager contributors, as still-worthwhile individuals seeking to maximize their human potential.[3] They complain that their prisons, however, provide insufficient opportunities for them to develop fully.

Burt made this point when discussing his past work as a dentist. His expertise, he thought, might be put to some good use, particularly given his long sentence:

BURT: When I first came to prison, I was so naive about the whole thing, so my expectations were that they'd put me to good use in some capacity. I have to spend all this time here; I would very much want to be a contributor, but—

HERBERT: As a dentist?

BURT: Yeah, or anything related health-wise. I've said I would be on a dental kind of committee or whatnot, even though I've heard so much how they function, that they go through the motions but there isn't so much substance to what they do. But anyway, again, that's my opinion and speculation, too.

HERBERT: But that avenue was closed to you?

BURT: And they haven't approached me to be on anything. My hearing has been a problem; it's a little less so now with the new hearing aid. But they're just not interested in—that's the feeling I get—in really paving the way for betterment of inmates and necessarily really hearing what you have to say.

Edgar raised an identical concern but extended it to consider the broad swath of contributions that easy keepers could make if allowed to do so. He envisioned a prison environment with the greater freedoms necessary to allow a flourishing of the human capital that otherwise lies latent in the easy-keeper community:

EDGAR: Well, I think that if you're incarcerated and you've got life without, that if you're doing [well] and you're staying out of trouble, that they should have a facility that you can go to that is a little more open—and gives you the ability to do things, as far as maybe schooling—and a little more free. Because you are doing life, this is it. It's not like you're going home in a couple months or something, so that you can fall into your life and have a life instead of just doing life. And the thing is, you've got that group of people. And now this group of people that you have at this institution, they're all doing [a] lengthy amount of time, but it's not a lockdown situation. You open up programs [so] that they can do things that are beneficial and contribute to society on a pretty good scale across the board. A lot of stuff. And they would. And then what it does is allow people like yourself to see more of the decent side of those types of people, and when parole comes up and stuff like that, then they have something to show the qualities of—you know what I mean? There's just none of that around; it's just not happening.

HERBERT: So somebody might say, "Well, he's got LWOP, why would we invest a cent more than we have to?"

EDGAR: Well, because we can contribute—and to a high degree— some real beneficial stuff. And there's the thing: if you're gonna be somewhere a long time, you can do a lot more than a guy that's not gonna be. And you can do it on a steady consistency. Could be a contributor. Instead of draining the system, you can contribute.

One place where lifers would like to contribute is the broader community of which they are a part. Many of them expressed

frustration at the barriers that denied them more regular interaction with those on the outside. Many wished that they could
provide some form of direct atonement for their misdeeds by
playing a constructive role in community betterment. They also
expressed an interest in helping those on the outside realize that
even individuals convicted of serious, violent crimes were not
beyond redemption.

Victor, for instance, spoke favorably about a previous prison
that housed him, one where greater connections to the outside
were fostered:

> They showed a lot of stuff with the community, community com-
> ing in to do a lot of stuff. They had a cancer walk, where a couple of
> cancer survivors came from the streets to walk on the weekend.
> That shows the community supporting you, actually seeing: "Hey,
> you know these people out here still think I'm human, that I'm
> okay." You have people doing that, you have people coming to take
> time off their schedule, come talk to us about what they do. People
> come help with programs for families at the visiting room, stuff like
> that.

Many lifers hoped for programs that would help with their
own needs. For some, this meant the greater availability of programs that might help them address underlying addiction issues
with which they had wrestled in the past. In general terms,
many lifers expressed a desire for prisons that more comprehensively addressed the emotional and physical trauma that had
characterized their pasts, and which had led to their criminal
behavior. Said one inmate, Isaac, "I wish that they had more
intelligent COs, that can deal with people in a therapeutic sense.
And comprehensively."

Others wished for chances to reckon more seriously with the
consequences of their past actions. Both Victor and Fred had

been in courses designed to accomplish precisely that. Both spoke of the power of the experience and the need to make it more widely available.

Victor's course was focused on redemption, and it asked participants to speak as openly as they could about the circumstances in which their crime was committed. For Victor, the degree of humanity that was revealed in the process shifted his personal perspective considerably:

> VICTOR: When I did the redemption class, that one kind of helped me out a little bit.
>
> HERBERT: How so?
>
> VICTOR: It just let me see that everybody's human. That everybody's human, and even if you're a prisoner or whatever, things change and there is a lot of forgiveness. Stuff like that. It opened my eyes up better and let me see that everybody's almost the same. You just have to give them a chance. We did little programs in there, where we shared stuff with each other; and a lot of people were in the same shoes I was in. And I was just waiting to hear that story, and as soon as they opened up, then nobody looked at them like: "Oh, look at that guy, he's weak." Everybody supported them, and I'm like: "Oh, that gave me a chance to open myself up."

As noted in chapter 1, Fred was in a restorative justice class. He was required to listen to crime victims, whose dire experiences led him to reconsider the consequences of his past actions. The class, he said, changed him profoundly, and thus he wondered if others might have a similar experience if such programs were more common:

> You take all of the white boys that are on this Nazi shit: if they were forced somehow or another to face some of the Holocaust victims, I think maybe that would change them and put a new slant on

things for them. And if some of these fucking dummies that run by, drive by, people at forty miles an hour and shoot the place up, if they had to face one of them kids they put in a wheelchair for life ... Those kinds of programs would make such a difference, I think. I mean, you'd have to be a rock not to be affected by that.

Yet Fred was hardly sanguine about the likelihood of any dramatic shift in how his prison was structured. He recognized too well that his institution was largely driven to ensure daily security. This meant presuming the worst about the prisoners and acting accordingly. For Fred, this only heightened the chances that misbehavior would result:

> When you run a punitive model like this, these guys—because you're dealing with the kind of people, me included, that are probably not the brightest people on the planet—when you put them in that position, they blow up on it. Like: "Okay, I'm a bad guy, and I'm gonna show you what a bad guy is." Those kinds of thoughts run through most of these dudes. If you were able to somehow get that barrier broken out a little bit—and I know they've got their security issues and all of that, and that's fine—there are so many other little programs they could do to start making a difference and chip away at that shit. I don't know if anyone is going to be able to get them to see the light on that, because they're locked in, they're dug in on their position. Yeah, and it seems like they're fortifying it daily.[4]

Fred's desire to see a less punitive prison was shared by his fellow easy keepers. They yearned for ample chances to demonstrate their creative and altruistic potential; they hoped that they could engage constructively with various social groups, both inside and outside prison. They hoped, in short, that the imperative to ensure safe custody could be relaxed in appropriate circumstances to allow greater flourishing. This arguable need to reconsider the regimes of custody emerges in even starker relief when one considers the consequences for prisons that house an increasingly large population of aging inmates.

"WELL, IT'S CUSTODY'S HOUSE": BALANCING SECURITY AND CARE

Like many medical professionals, Fiona had practiced her craft elsewhere before becoming a prison nurse. She quickly learned that some of her professional habits would need to change. In particular, she discovered that concerns about security were paramount. She used the story of an incident that occurred early in her prison career to illustrate the point:

> Well, it's custody's house, and then it's medicine within that construct. And a perfect example is when I was brand new here. I had had some home help experience; and when you see a medical emergency, you call 911 and you do what you need to, to get that patient to the hospital. That's what I was used to doing. So, as a brand new nurse here, that's what I did. I picked up the phone, called 911, and 911 arrived. But the problem is: in order to send someone off the hill, you have to have trip orders. You have to assemble a trip team of two officers. You have to change the guy out, get him in his orange jumpsuit: they do a strip search, they get him in the chains and all the garb. And then the two officers have to go with that offender to the hospital with the 911 crew. I wasn't used to having to coordinate that custody piece of it to get somebody to the hospital, where they needed to go. So, there was a learning curve.

This concern about safety is certainly understandable. Prisons can be dangerous places, and thus custody staff develop and practice routines that seek to minimize the possibility of violence. For medical staff, that means learning new sets of rules. For Hettie, a nurse, the biggest change was managing the space and content of her interactions with patients: "Boundaries are huge, you know? We don't share certain things, obviously, with the inmates, because we're the staff. Personal space, standing a certain distance from the inmates, our environment—watching out for our environment, looking around, scanning our environment. Talking to inmates—communicating, collaborating, reporting, all of that."

Although medical staff may not enter the prison world with the same concerns as the custody staff, they are taught to make adjustments. As Hettie notes, this certainly means interacting with prisoners differently than they would patients on the outside. This can be an abrupt transition for many, especially when treating older inmates. Carly, a veteran nurse, had seen other nurses struggle with this reality: "You don't touch offenders or patients, offender-patients, unless you are specifically doing a procedure. There's no patting. There's no touching. There's no relating personal experiences. Especially when you see these grandparent-age people, I think, particularly younger-age nursing staff have a hard time making that transition. We do this for a reason.... We have to render care with respect and to the best of our ability. But you leave out all the personal touches. That's hard."[5]

Medical staff indicate that managing the potential tension between security and care is not necessarily a frequent issue. Yet there are instances when the tension does make itself felt.[6] Carly herself noted this: "Sometimes, there's a conflict between fundamental beliefs. I think I've seen it a lot. You as an officer may think this is a scumbag guy. Me, I see him as a patient. If you come to work and you have a bad attitude, or somebody yelled at you, or whatever, then you may, perhaps unconsciously, translate that into slowing your care down even further, because you can. There is a direct impact." The most jarring instance of this conflict, Carly said, was when a custody officer wondered aloud why she had bothered to respond to a prisoner in a life-threatening situation: "You know, I had an officer one time ask me why I saved somebody. That's my job. That's why I'm here." As she later emphasized, "It's not our job to punish them. It's our job to provide care. The same thing with custody. It's their job to provide safety and security, not to punish. The courts already punished them."

Conversations with staff indicate that potential conflicts between custody and care will likely magnify as the population of aging prisoners increases.[7] As prisoners grow old, their needs will necessarily multiply. As they lose cognitive and physical abilities, their capacity for self-care will deteriorate. The caretaking responsibilities for all staff—medical staff and custody staff alike—will proliferate. This is a reality that custody officers can be expected to struggle to accommodate, according to many staff. As Ike, a doctor, noted,

> It's the officers that actually have to go into the cell or move the offender or untie him from the ceiling, whatever. And they kind of anticipate: "Oh, I see another problem coming. And I'm going to have to give him CPR. Do you really have to have him here, because I'm just looking at him and I can tell I'll catch something." We have devices for it and, yes, he's right, he would have to give CPR. We all would. So we have to let the officers know, because there are certain things that the officers would have to tolerate more of than we usually do.

Of particular concern to many is how custody staff can and will handle prisoners whose dementia alters their behavior.[8] For some such prisoners, this will mean they are incontinent. For others, it can mean fits of unprovoked violence. A particularly challenging case noted by Greg, a doctor, was when both problems manifested themselves in a single prisoner: "Some guys, when they get dementia, they become placid. Others become very aggressive. We had a guy up in our inpatient unit: he was swinging right and left every time you went to change his diaper. You had to have two or three officers in there. And even though you talk very calmly to him, he's unpredictable. He'll often slug you without you even knowing it's coming. Some guys really give you a hard time, but they still need the care." Ike had a similarly harrowing story:

> We make as many accommodations as we can, but it can be very, very difficult if a person is too incontinent. There have been cases where it brought us to our knees. We had a guy that was incontinent with urine and feces. Sometimes he would lose his stool in the shower, which created all sorts of problems, because the showers are shared by many other people: it's a biohazard. So it's a major challenge when we have a severely problematic aging offender, and they may be struggling with all the things I've described and be fifty or sixty—and of course, still have thirty or fifty more years left on their sentence. So they're not going anywhere.

Ralph, a senior custody officer, recognized that many in his charge will likely need some help to properly interpret the behavior of some of the prisoners suffering from dementia, particularly if occasional violence occurs: "Those offenders probably aren't intentionally trying to hurt people or act out—it's the disease. It's probably a challenge to get staff to understand that and not think that they're trying to hurt them. That it's the disease that's making them act the way they do. Probably, staff education would be a bit of a challenge."

Another challenge for custody staff is how best to make accommodations when necessary for impaired prisoners. Such accommodations can disrupt typical routines, which are one of the chief means by which custody staff seek to maximize safety. Prisoners are regulated through set practices: movement is controlled, possessions are limited, counts and searches are common.

But these routines presume an able-bodied, cognitively functioning prisoner. If a prisoner is ailing, custody staff may need to step outside regular practices, which is not always easy. Dick, a veteran officer, described the challenges he faces when he must take a wheelchair-using prisoner to an off-site medical visit. This presents a dilemma, because prison rules require a strip search whenever an inmate will encounter someone from outside the prison: "Let's say I want to strip-search an inmate before he goes out on a medical trip. Okay, we take him, for example, to the infirmary, where the restroom is, and he's in a wheelchair. What we'll do is—I call them power strips. There are these silver bars that they have on each side of the toilet. That's where we do the strip search, so the inmate can use those to assist us in terms of doing the strip search. So you gotta be able to accommodate those things."

Mark was a classification counselor who had previously worked as a custody officer. He was thus able to recognize that declining prisoners have increased needs, but also how custody staff struggle as special, nonroutine adjustments become necessary:

> MARK: For instance, medical may say this guy needs oxygen in his
> nose, so we would have to go through the approval process.
> Superintendent would have to approve for that device to be
> kept at the offender's cell, make notifications to all of our unit
> staff—the sergeants, the lieutenants—so that they know that
> this guy has this device in his cell. Or he may have taken it to
> the dayroom; he may need oxygen all of the time. It's not
> bottles of oxygen: it's just a machine that does it for him,
> oxygenates it. So communication is one of the biggest things
> there is.

HERBERT: So, oxygenators. What other kind of medical accommodations might you have to make?

MARK: Maybe the guy needs a cane—you know, just a simple cane. But you look at the cane and think: What could that be used for? Could it hurt? Absolutely. Could it be taken away from him and somebody else use it? Absolutely. Those are some things we consider also. Let's say a guy needs some back support, so we're gonna give him a piece of foam up there on his bed so he's sitting up a little bit, instead of lying flat. Again that's another approval process—notifications, so we know that guy can have that in his cell, nobody else.

HERBERT: Interesting. So does this create issues for the custody staff?

MARK: Well, it could. Because you know: This guy was issued it. Or was he? Well, he just had it ... Where'd it go? Somebody strong-armed him for it: "You're gonna give it to me." "No, I got it for myself." So now the staff gonna get up and deal with this guy: "Hey, you took this. How'd you get it?" "Oh, he just gave it to me." So now we gotta figure out what's going on between those two guys. Is there a threat to this guy? Do we gotta lock this guy up in segregation? So that one simple thing, like, "Here, just take it," on the outside—well, on the inside, it could be used as a tool.

As Mark indicates, custody may be understandably devoted to set procedures, but the needs of aging prisoners will require uncomfortable adaptations. Greg told a particularly compelling story to illustrate how customary practices can seem remarkably jarring when imposed on cognitively compromised prisoners. He was describing prisoners incarcerated for a sex offense. Many such prisoners are housed at Twin Rivers, because one of its units is dedicated to those who undergo sex offender treatment. This treatment is required for those convicted of sex offenses, as they near the end of their sentences. But prisoners suffering from dementia were better suited, Greg thought, to the Sage Unit, at another prison, Coyote Ridge Corrections Center, located in central Washington. That unit is dedicated to prisoners who need assistance with their daily needs. But the treatment requirement for sex offenders meant that cognitively impaired prisoners were commonly housed at Twin Rivers, which frustrated Greg: "That's why it's a real problem if you need to be here for sex offender treatment and they're not capable of getting around. Somebody who really should be in the Sage Unit—a senior, assisted-living unit—has got to be here for sex offender treatment. You've got a guy that can't remember what he ate yesterday. And he's trying to take this program because it's required before he gets out."

Of course, there are arguably better means to manage the tensions between custody concerns and bureaucratic routines, on the one hand, and the demands of an aging prisoner population, on the other. One such means is to construct more prison facilities along the lines of a nursing home, so that impaired prisoners can be more easily accommodated. This was a possibility raised by a wide number of the staff.

At the time of our interview, Angela, a counselor, had just completed her own research on life-sentenced prisoners housed at the institution where she worked. Her analysis had demonstrated to her the pressing medical needs that aging prisoners were steadily accumulating. She recognized that her prison, more than a century old, was beyond poorly equipped to provide a comfortable existence for declining prisoners. She wondered aloud whether the state of Washington was allowing elderly prisoners to live in conditions that it would not tolerate elsewhere:

I don't know what [proper facilities for elderly prisoners] would
look like, but how do we handle people in the community with
dementia? How do we handle people in the community that are
elderly and can't live alone anymore? Do we stick them in a metal
box? On a metal bed? How do we handle them? You have somebody
who's eighty-five years old that's been incarcerated for twenty to
thirty years on a mattress that's yea thick [holds finger and thumb a
short distance apart], and then you wonder why he has back issues.
It's not playing favorites, but it's a matter of maintaining a life.
They are a ward of the state, so how are we going to address that?

Elderly prisoners are, staff suggested, frequently distressed in
their unforgiving prison environments. Part of the issue, as
Angela indicated, is their physical comfort. An additional issue
is their social comfort. Without an opportunity to be in a facility tailored to their needs, they are housed in units with many
younger, louder, and occasionally predatory inmates. This generates much discomfort, according to Carl, a counselor: "They'll
tell you that: 'I'm eighty years old, and I'm here with these
youngsters.' Those are the guys, the older guys; they are the
guys you see kind of hanging in their cell all day. That's what I
see on my caseload."

Finding alternate locales for such prisoners is a challenge.
Carly, a nurse, described the common process that ensues when
staff discern emerging dementia in an inmate:

We start this round of: "Okay, here's what's wrong. Where can they
go? Okay, no, they can't go there. Okay, what about this? Okay, no.
What about that?" We have sent a couple people with really significant dementia over to SOU.[9] They then live in a block cell. That's
not the answer either, but we don't have wards for dementia and
Alzheimer's. We have mental health and we have medical. Again,
over at Sage, they take a lot of these guys. As we get older, that is
the question. We need money, because we need to build facilities.

Many staff described their desire to see numerous prisoners who are held in Monroe housed instead at the Sage Unit.[10] However, the Sage Unit, as noted in chapter 3, houses only individuals who are classified as minimum security. This means that very few life-sentenced prisoners can move there. Further, Sage struggles to accommodate individuals whose dementia leads them to erratic and perhaps violent behavior. This reality frustrated staff like Ike: "The problem with Sage is that they can't take all custody levels. So it only helps a limited number of people. Their custody status has to be okay, everything has to be okay. And then they could possibly go there if they're well behaved. But it's a bit of an oxymoron to say that a criminally involved Alzheimer's patient is gonna be well behaved. So they need to learn—they need more capacity, more staffing. And sometimes [inmates] can be medicated to the point where they're near stupor. That's just not usual care."

More usual care, many staff suggested, could only result in facilities specifically designed for the aged. Belinda, a psychologist, was especially eloquent in outlining this need:

At some point this state and other states have to consider units for the elderly. What does that really look like, and do they put people [there] that are elderly—not to label them—but for their safety? Maybe they all reside in one unit, and what does that look like? What do those services look like? ADA cells—maybe it looks a little different. I would imagine that would be very expensive, because you have to decide at some point: what's your health care plan, and what does it cover as people age in the system? I don't know what the offender health care plan covers in that way. I think it will definitely be an issue. I would imagine that a special pod or unit or area would definitely be needed. I don't think we have a hospice unit or area. I think those are definitely global decisions that will have to be addressed as one issue in the future, because there will be more people getting older.

Regardless of whether new facilities arise or not, the costs of maintaining an aging population will mount considerably. Several staff pointed to this issue as they considered the future. Many emphasized that they are already short of staff and financial resources and were worried about a future in which many more prisoners needed even greater attention. Prisoners incapable of attending to all of their daily needs, who are undergoing particularly complicated medical treatment, whose medication regime is extensive and complicated, who wish for a death with some measure of comfort and support—all of these require significant commitments of resources. Many will need trips to outside medical facilities for specialized care, and those who stay in hospitals must be attended by a custody officer. As Paul put it, in his role in coordinating these outside trips: "I've seen up to ten hospital watches going at the same time, so if you can imagine that—ten officers out on different hospitals, twenty-four hours a day for the duration of those stays. That gets pretty spendy pretty quick. A majority of that is overtime."

Costs will also attend medications and in-house staff, who must try to meet the daily needs of declining prisoners. Greg commented, "I think we'll have a lot more guys that need durable medical equipment. I think we'll have a lot more pushers, a lot more assistants, a lot more therapeutic mattresses to prevent skin breakdown on our paraplegics, quadriplegics. I mean, you take a quadriplegic, and you've got your hands full. It's a lot to ask of nursing to take care of five to ten of those guys."

In the future, of course, there will be more than five to ten such prisoners in many facilities. For this reason, current punishment policy appears to mandate an increasing number of institutions to better manage the potential tension between custody and care. If prisoners debilitated by age and by various medical conditions are to be housed with any degree of humane care, states like Washington simply must build nursing-home-style facilities to accommodate them.

Yet there is another option. Perhaps our punishment policy could change, so that life-sentenced prisoners—and especially easy keepers—can be more readily released from prison.

"I'M JUST HERE": ON THE NEED TO RECONSIDER PUNISHMENT POLICY

Melvin was proud of the work he did around the prison. He worked a steady job and used all available opportunities to counsel younger prisoners. He stayed in steady communication with the various members of his family and tried earnestly to help support them, both financially and emotionally. He avoided trouble and was viewed by both staff and prisoners as the quintessential easy keeper. Given his productivity, he saw little utility in his sentence: "I'm just here. They spend forty-two thousand dollars a year on me, just to be here. I don't get in any kind of trouble, there's no disciplinary stuff. I'm out there, my mind is out there. It's a waste, especially when you see the kids going hungry, the elderly going without. And they spend forty-two thousand dollars a year on me?"

Melvin thought his prison was filled with inmates with similarly pointless sentences. As their capacities diminished, their already-limited world shrank to the barest of minimums: a life largely confined to a tiny cell, with limited activity and social interaction:

> Honestly, they're sitting there waiting to die. They talk about death row and death penalty, but there's no difference, there's not. We get to move around a little more, some, but there's some that

don't—they gave up. So it's no different, they're just sitting there waiting to die. I have life without. Like I said, I know I'm not the only one that sees that and thinks that stuff—you have no choice but to think of it, no matter how busy you keep yourself. And maybe that's why a lot of us stay that way, to try to keep our mind off that stuff. Because it takes a hold. Even me, with the support that I have and everything that I have going. And after you do so much time, we're just here. There's a lot of us, there's just nothing more you can get out of us. There's not. We don't get in trouble, we're just here.

What rankles many lifers is the complete absence of either incentives or rewards for their positive behavior. Even as they work steadily to improve the institutions that house them, they do so with barely any recognition of their good deeds. With no hope for these lifers' release, their contributions cannot influence a parole board or other agency that might provide some form of reward. They can move to a prison with minimum restrictions only under the rarest of circumstances, and only if they are clearly beset with dementia. While they are able-bodied and steadily productive, their efforts gain no recognition. Nate observed, "Well, really, if you do their sentence like they want you to do, I'd be just sitting in the cell rotting, just eating goodies and watching TV or whatever. Or going to the yard or whatever. There's no emphasis on bettering yourself with prison. There really isn't. There is none. I mean, once you do, pat on the back maybe. Or they'll say, 'Well that's what you're supposed to be doing.'"

After a while, many declining prisoners slide into lassitude, worn down by the burdens of routine and boredom. With a sense of humor dripping with cynicism, Gerald assessed his predicament:

GERALD: It's just monotonous in here, man. I'm just—like I said, I'm old and I'm tired of that. I'm old and I'm tired. I picked a hell of a time to get tired and get stuck up in here with all these idiots. But I'm old, and I'm tired. That's the only way I can say it. I'm old, and I'm tired. Don't get me wrong—when I was young, some of that stuff was kinda exciting and fun, just doin' things that you ain't supposed to be doin', especially when you're stuck in one of these places. You know what I'm saying?

HERBERT: So, from your perspective, the state of Washington has gotten enough from you?

GERALD: Yeah. Yeah. Oh, no doubt. I feel that, anyways. They'll probably put that on my tombstone. That I still owe 'em some time.

That the state of Washington demands more time from those who are clearly disabled is an especially jarring reality for easy keepers. The fearsome image of a criminal predator who deserves life in prison is starkly contradicted by a graying inmate too feeble to propel his wheelchair without help. Said Thomas,

> Personally, I don't see any benefit to me or to society by putting anyone in prison at eighty years old. And I see guys now that are older, and they are in wheelchairs and strollers and all kinds of stuff. I don't know if they were that way when they came in, or they became that way after they arrived. I'm not sure. But I think that the probability of them reoffending would be really small.[11] It costs the state a lot of money to take care of these people in normal conditions, and now they have to spend more because of their situations in their life.

While still able-bodied, most easy keepers do good works because it enables them to feel like contributors, like people trying to rebuild their lives despite past misdeeds. They seek to atone for their crimes, to be more productive and purposeful as a contrast to the destruction they previously wrought. This sentiment was expressed by many of those I interviewed. Nate was especially eloquent on this point:

> HERBERT: So, as you look back on the crime that you committed, do you feel like some measure of atonement is important for you to perform?
>
> NATE: Yeah. I think the only thing that I can do is help rebuild. Because I've done nothing but destroy. If you think about the gang lifestyle, if you think about just selling drugs in general: You're destroying a lot. You're destroying not only just trust, you're destroying other people's lives. And having no boundaries on what you do to get money—it's just not a good way to live at all. I think the only thing that I can do to make up for that is try to deter people from going down that road, and use my influence—instead of for negative as I used to—for positive. I think that's the best thing I can do. And that's what I continue to do. Because I feel like I'm giving back. I don't think that I'll ever atone completely—I think it's gonna be a lifetime thing for me to devote my life to the opposite way.

Like many other easy keepers, Leonard firmly believed that his personal transformation was complete. He was convinced that his orientation toward life and toward others was fully changed from when he first entered prison at eighteen:

> I've already become the man that I want to be. If there's something that I really want to do, I just go for it. I don't need to be guided in that way, because whatever it is that I do, it's going to be a positive thing. I don't need to be convinced of that or given advice on how to do a certain thing, because before I tackle anything, I think a lot about it. It's always going to be something good. Something decent. Maybe not extraordinary, but not ordinary either. A lot of times people wait to see something extraordinary happen. Waiting for

something extraordinary to happen in their lives before they get out and do something. Our whole lives are going to be full of ordinary moments, and every once in a while we might be able to make something extraordinary out of those ordinary moments. I think that's everybody's goal, right? To make a difference in some way, somehow, whether it's on a huge scale or a small scale. We want to make a difference.

Yet as much difference as Leonard and other easy keepers are able to make, both their contributions and transformations remain largely unrecognized. To find such neglect, one need look no further than many of the staff members at the prisons that house them. Even those staffers who express considerable appreciation for the easy keepers who made their institutions run more smoothly still balked at the idea that any of them should be released. Mark, for example, a veteran custody officer, frowned on the concept:

MARK: Yeah, they're here, and they're easier keepers. They're the ones who encourage the younger offenders to get into school, get into programs. In a sense, they try to mentor the younger offenders, and in my eyes they're actually a benefit to the facility.

HERBERT: They would say that their works suggest that they deserve to get out—some of them.

MARK: Just because someone has changed and don't get in trouble in prison—mainly because they don't have the opportunity that they would [have] once they're out in the community. Because we try to keep everything so structured, so they don't have those opportunities. You got a—and this is just a hypothetical—serial rapist who goes to prison. Okay, he hasn't raped anybody for ten years. That's because he's in prison. That doesn't mean that he's changed and won't do it again once he gets out.

Or here's Ralph, another long-serving member of the custody staff:

RALPH: Like I said, they're pretty easy keepers.

HERBERT: Are they so easy that maybe they don't need to be here anymore?

RALPH: No, they need to be here. Some of the crimes they've done are pretty horrific, pretty bad crimes. There's guys that should never get out just because of the notoriety of their crime. When you have some cold-blooded murderers, that just murder people ruthless—those guys, no matter how good they've been in prison, are not likely to get released.

These arguments by Mark and Ralph merit challenge. It is certainly the case that many life-sentenced prisoners committed horrific crimes, and that some of them may reoffend if they are released.[12] But this hardly eliminates the reality that many easy keepers have changed irrevocably for the better and thus deserve consideration for release.

Prison staff are not uniformly immune to such merciful sentiments. Medical staff, for instance, are notably more likely to express some compassion for lifers and other prisoners. Ike, for instance, recognized the ongoing need to help himself and others see prisoners as more than just individuals who committed criminal acts: "Nobody goes into nursing just to clean up diapers of a convicted rapist. It's just—you know. So part of my job is also to highlight other important things about the patient. Like: he is a patient, he is somebody's father, somebody's grandfather. He is something—you gotta reframe, because he needs you right now. So he needs the best nurse he can have, and right now that's you." Medical staff appear able to recognize that they are, in fact, among the few public servants from whom many prisoners can expect care. This is most poignantly evident when prisoners near death. Terminally stricken individuals outside of prison can take comfort in hospice or other care that is designed to reduce their pain and maximize their comfort. In prison, such luxuries are absent. As Carly put it,

> When someone is going to die and it's long-term, and we know, they don't go to an in-patient hospice outside. One, nobody wants them. That's the reality of these guys. Nobody wants them. What was happening at one time was [that] a social worker and a nurse were coming to the fourth-floor hospital. I think they were coming once every two weeks. Or once a week, or something. But it didn't work. Even though someone is sick or dying, they live in a cell. That's what the rooms on the fourth floor are. They're cells. Some of the things we would do for people at hospice at home—with massive amounts of meds, because there's always somebody there, to be right there with them—it doesn't work so great in our system. We do great hospice work, but these are the things you have to consider as you're doing it.

Perhaps because they bear the brunt of caring for the infirm and terminally ill, medical staff appear more likely to recognize the necessity of releasing easy keepers. Adrian was a medical administrator who daily confronted the rising costs of care for elderly prisoners. Such costs, he believed, simply mandated the need for the state of Washington to reconsider its opposition to parole:

> I come from the idea that what the state would probably benefit from, in the correctional system, is to get a parole system. I don't see how we can stay away from that in the long term. I understand public safety, and we want to ensure that people take responsibility for their crimes, but we definitely need to take into consideration the costs associated and the chances that they can get better treatment if they were on parole. So I *think* we will move in that direction in the future, I would anticipate. If not, then they're going to have to increase the budget, increase staffing, just to meet the needs of the offenders medically.

Lifers also fear this emerging reality. They hardly wish to grow old and die in prison. They witness others declining—physically, cognitively, emotionally. Beyond decrying such a fate, many lifers wonder what public good is served in the process. William remarked, "I'm getting older, and when I see old men eighty years old in here—it's appalling, in my mind. Because what can an eighty-year-old man do? Besides get abused in prison? That sometimes comes to my mind. If anything, I say to myself, 'Please don't let me get old like that. I can't do anything. Don't let me get fragile to the point that guys have to push me around." And there's a lot of abuse goes on in here when people get old."

Lifers see little humane rationale for such an outcome. They cannot find justification for a punishment that denies the possibility that their redemption can be recognized. Quite the opposite, they suggest: more can be obtained by seeing how transformations do, in fact, occur. Victor was eloquent on this point:

VICTOR: In terms of somebody getting life without parole, I don't think anybody should get life without parole.

HERBERT: Why not?

VICTOR: Because people change. People change, and there are other ways of punishing somebody. But I guess if I was in the other shoes, then it would be hard to say. But I wouldn't want to give somebody life without parole.

HERBERT: Again, why not?

VICTOR: It's just too much time. It's too much time, and it's not going to fix anything. I'm not going to get nobody back if somebody died. I'm not going to get that person back. That person is not going to be happy because that guy got life without parole. It doesn't solve anything. It might make the person feel better: "Oh, that guy got justice." But it's not justice. Because the person handing down the sentence is just as bad as the person that committed the crime, because they're ruining each other. He ruined the victim's life, and now the guy that is giving the prisoner the time is ruining his life.

Easy keepers work assiduously to avoid a ruined life. Despite the odds that they will suffer an unceremonious end—a lonely death in a spartan prison hospital—they still seek succor in a purposeful life. Their transformations are sufficiently thorough that they possess no doubts about their ability to avoid reoffending. Even as they acknowledge the pain caused by their past crimes, they still see little social benefit in their enduring confinement. It is obviously in their self-interest to be considered for release, but they make persuasive arguments that their increased access to parole would benefit society as a whole. Leonard made this point:

> I would start looking at people who have done a lot of time in prison. There has to be a way to determine if somebody's ready to go. I would focus on life people. I wish the life-without-parole sentence would go away, and that there would be some way to give them another opportunity, to get them out of the facilities. If that'd just change, there would be hundreds of people across the state that would be looked at that have done just a huge amount of time. I don't know much about the courts or the sentencing systems. So, I don't know how I would react to change in that, because I don't know enough about it. I just know that the current system doesn't seem to be working.

For himself, Leonard was quite clear about the needlessness of his continued residence in prison: "There's no reason they need to hold me here any longer. I'm not a perfect guy, but I'm not a danger to society. I'm not any kind of trouble at all. I'm a guy that committed a horrible crime when I was eighteen. I'm fifty-one now, and I would like to go home. I would. I really hope that something in the future does change to the point of allowing me to do that." That said, Leonard recognizes that there is risk attached to allowing him or any easy keeper to be released. Yet he simultaneously notes that there is little more he can do to demonstrate his transformation, and no way to entirely eliminate the risk of reoffending: "The only way to demonstrate that I would not reoffend is by proving it out in the community. Can't prove it in here anymore than I already have. I mean, I haven't had any write-ups forever. I've never been in a fight in prison. I've been working full time. There's not a staff member in here that would say anything bad about me, other than the fact that some staff just don't like prisoners. How would I prove that?"

CONCLUSION: ON THE NEED TO MOVE MOUNTAINS

Leonard's dilemma is shared by the rest of us. How *do* prisoners prove that they have changed? How *do* we determine who deserves release? How *do* we assess any effort at redemption? How *do* we become comfortable if convicted murderers like Leonard are allowed to live among us?

The easiest response to these questions is simply to avoid them, a strategy commonly embraced in the United States. Fear of crime has driven American politics to paroxysm and fueled polices that make the United States by far the world's leader in rates of incarceration. The rise of life-sentenced prisoners is a direct outcome of such policies. Easy keepers like Leonard thus accumulate inside prisons and watch forlornly as time marches forward.[13] Their good works, while notable and beneficial, lie unrecognized; their redemptive stories lack the wider readership they deserve.[14]

There is, of course, no simple way to reconstruct punishment policy. Parole systems, for instance, will hardly be infallible.

They are human-designed and -enacted processes, after all, ones that are necessarily affected by political currents. Such political currents almost always make it easier to keep lifers inside, even if their behavior demonstrates that they do not threaten public safety.[15]

This yearning for safety is understandable. It is even somewhat morally grounded. If Leonard committed murder, then perhaps his transgression must be met with a clear moral response. His life sentence is thus a just desert. Anything less might symbolically minimize the moral harm he caused. It might cheapen a victim's life if the sentence were shorter.

But this argument stands on unstable moral grounds. A just-deserts punishment policy can unjustifiably freeze people like Leonard in time and render him nothing other than the transgression he committed. Such an effacing of his human fallibility, and of his capacity for change, can hardly be described as moral.[16] A more humane policy—not to mention a more fiscally responsible one—would recognize his capacity for change.[17] Such a policy would also foster efforts at such change and would reward them when it occurs.

Indeed, the retributionist impulse at the core of a just-deserts policy need not be considered incompatible with either rehabilitation or mercy. Retribution compels a recognition of the debt the offender owes to society, and it demands recompense. A punishment thus is meant to send a clear moral message to the convict and to recalibrate a society damaged by the criminal transgression. The punishment should set the moral balance back aright.

If a moral balance is what we seek, easy keepers demonstrate its possibility. They hear the moral message their punishment conveys, and they use their resultant regret to motivate their good works. They deliberately strive to atone by working to prevent the moral harm that future criminality represents. Their investment in their younger, crime-prone peers is their best available means to repay the debt they recognize that they owe.[18] Such good works deserve recognition.

This was one of the points that Nate chose to emphasize. He suggested, first, that he was not inherently evil, despite his involvement with a gang-related murder of a young child. When asked about the more difficult aspects of his 134-year sentence, he said, "You know, realizing again that this person that my mom cherishes—how could I be sentenced to … how could I be an enemy of the state and she cherishes me so much? Something's wrong here; my mom doesn't have evil."

Nate's capacity for good, in his view, was something he enacted every day, through his work habits, his tutoring, his efforts to distinguish himself as a role model. Despite the satisfactions his good works provided, he felt constricted in his ability to fully atone: "I know I'll be so much more ready for the world now. I don't even have any doubts that I would know how to live and conduct myself like a regular citizen. And I feel that I have pretty much a debt to pay out there. Not in here—you know what I mean, out there."

Nate's most fervent wish was that he and his fellow easy keepers could be viewed through a prism that recognized the possibility for redemption. When asked about the most important thing that he would like to see changed in the prison that housed him, he did not hesitate: "It would be nice if they would say, 'You know what? Since we see that people can change, what we're gonna do, we're gonna start treating people as if they can change.' The belief that people have value and that they are redeemable. That alone would, I'm telling you, it would move mountains. It would move mountains."

That these mountains are not yet moving is hardly welcome news to easy keepers like Nate. Still, he remains undaunted: "What do you do? We have to try to make believers out of 'em. It seems like it's a never-ending battle, but that doesn't mean give up. And it may not change even in my lifetime, but you can't give up. 'Cause then you really have wasted your time. But I think sooner or later something's got to give. Something has to give."

If we allow room for such voices as Nate's, if we recognize the value of their stories, if we bear witness to the redemptive scripts they etch each day in purposeful activity, we can find ample reasons to agree that, indeed, something has to give. Even if thousands of life sentences provide us some measure of increased security, they come at a terrible price, both fiscally and morally.[19]

It is well beyond time that we collectively eased up on the easy keepers we so readily confine. A more humane and fiscally responsible punishment regime awaits just such a policy reconsideration. Easy keepers vivify so many of the values that we hold dear—altruism, civic responsibility, hard work, reliability—that their continued confinement represents a stain on our collective morality. We should make it much harder to keep them so easily.

Notes

INTRODUCTION

1. LWOP is an acronym for "life without parole." Some of the quotes in this book have been lightly edited for clarity.

2. As with all of the interviewees quoted in this manuscript, this is a pseudonym.

3. Leonard is referring to extended family visits. These are opportunities for prisoners to spend time overnight with family members in a trailer on the prison grounds.

4. John Irwin writes that lifers are "an important presence in the convict world and constitute a body of elder statesmen. They are sought out for advice and relied upon as go-betweens in conflicts between prisoners and between prisoners and staff." John Irwin, *The Warehouse Prison: Disposal of the New Dangerous Class* (Los Angeles: Roxbury, 2005).

5. Ashley Nellis, *Still Life: America's Increasing Use of Life and Long-Term Sentences* (Washington, DC: Sentencing Project, 2017), p. 5. In this analysis, Nellis combines those who have life sentences with those who have "virtual life" sentences (scheduled release dates that exceed their expected life spans). Nellis does not distinguish between life-sentenced prisoners who are eligible for parole and those who are not. In the state of Washington, parole was abolished in the mid-1980s. For

that reason, a significant percentage of its life-sentenced population, including the twenty-one individuals I interviewed, foresee no possibility for release.

6. Catherine Appleton and Bent Grover noted in a 2007 analysis that, at that time, the ratio of the life-without-parole population to the U.S. prison population as a whole had increased a hundredfold over the previous thirty years. That ratio today would be even higher. Catherine Appleton and Bent Grover, "The Pros and Cons of Life Imprisonment," *British Journal of Criminology* 47 (2007): 602.

7. Nellis, *Still Life*, p. 19. Human Rights Watch calculated that the number of life-sentenced prisoners in the United States grew ninety-four times faster than the total sentenced-prisoner population in the period between 2007 and 2010 alone. Human Rights Watch, *Old behind Bars: The Aging Prison Population in the United States* (New York: Human Rights Watch, 2012), p. 6.

8. American Civil Liberties Union, *At America's Expense: The Mass Incarceration of the Elderly* (Washington, DC: ACLU, 2012), p. i.

9. On the rampant racial disparities throughout the American criminal justice process, see Ashley Nellis, *The Color of Justice: Racial and Ethnic Disparity in Prisons* (Washington, DC: Sentencing Project, 2016); Samuel Walker, Cassia Spohn, and Miriam Delone, *The Color of Justice: Race, Ethnicity and Crime in America* (Boston: Cengage, 2011); Michael Tonry, *Punishing Race* (Oxford: Oxford University Press, 2011). On the proportion of African Americans in the U.S. lifer population, see Nellis, *Still Life*, p. 14.

10. Ibid.

11. Harvard Law Review Association, "A Matter of Life and Death: The Effect of Life-without-Parole Statutes on Capital Punishment," *Harvard Law Review* 119 (2006): 1838–1854.

12. Ashley Nellis, *Life Goes On: The Historic Rise of Life Sentences in America*. (Washington, DC: Sentencing Project, 2013). Of course, not all life sentences eliminate the possibility of parole. Indeed, the number of persons with a sentence of life with the possibility of parole is about twice the number of those serving life without. However, the granting of parole has declined considerably in recent years. As a consequence, life-sentenced prisoners who do get parole serve significantly longer terms than they did in the past. See Nazgol Ghandnoosh, *Delaying a*

Second Chance: The Declining Prospects for Parole on Life Sentences (Washington, DC: Sentencing Project, 2017).

13. Marie Gottschalk, "Sentenced to Life: Penal Reform and the Most Severe Sanctions," *Annual Review of Law and Social Science* 9 (2013): 353–382.

14. For a review of the various policies that generated the massive growth in life sentences, see Human Rights Watch, *Old behind Bars;* Nellis, *Still Life.*

15. On these political developments, see Katherine Beckett, *Making Crime Pay: Law and Order in Contemporary American Politics* (Oxford: Oxford University Press, 1997); Jonathan Simon, *Governing through Crime: How the War on Crime Transformed American Democracy and Created a Culture of Fear* (Oxford: Oxford University Press, 2009).

16. National Research Council, *The Growth of Incarceration in the United States: Exploring Causes and Consequences* (Washington, DC: National Academies Press, 2014); Nellis, *Life Goes On.*

17. Nellis, *Still Life.*

18. Ibid.

19. Nellis, *Life Goes On.* Marie Gottschalk notes that violent offenders accounted for 60 percent of the growth in the size of the state prison population from 2000 to 2008. During this period, the number of sentenced drug offenders in state prisons actually declined by 8 percent. Marie Gottschalk, *Caught: The Prison State and the Lockdown of American Politics* (Princeton, NJ: Princeton University Press, 2015), p. 214.

20. Ghandnoosh, *Delaying a Second Chance.*

21. All of the individuals I interviewed were men. This is sensible, because men constitute more than 95 percent of those with a life sentence. See Nellis, *Still Life.*

22. Subjects were recruited through a staged process. Initially, staff at each prison scheduled a session to which all life-sentenced prisoners were invited. I used that group meeting to describe the research and to distribute copies of both the interview questions and the consent form that each interviewee would be required to sign. Prisoners who were interested in being interviewed were subsequently asked to send a note to their counselor. Once I had the list of interested prisoners, I selected a sample of participants to best approximate the racial composition of Washington's lifer population as a whole.

23. According to Nellis, in 2016, the racial composition of lifers in Washington was as follows: 69.5 percent white, 17.2 percent African American, 12.8 percent Latinx, and 0.5 percent other. Nellis, *Still Life*, p. 15.

24. All told, forty-eight different undergraduates—all majors in the Department of Law, Societies, and Justice at the University of Washington—provided transcription labor for this project. They are too numerous to mention individually, but their work was stellar, selfless, and much appreciated.

25. One of the lifers I interviewed, Henry, described how the lifers in his institution learn quickly that they need to be positive forces, not negative ones. Describing an individual who enters his prison with a poor attitude, he said, "Yeah. You might come in with that attitude, but you have to make a decision real quick because the people that are lifers don't want to be around anybody like that. We don't want to be around that negativity. We'll do what we can to help that person. Try to get them thinking differently and help them with the process of beginning this life sentence, but in this institution in particular, those type of people are not here, in regards to lifers. They're not in this institution. If they want to live that way, there's close custody for them. There's other places for them. This is not the prison for that. This is the place to be positive. This is the place to be creative. This is the place to heal. This is the place to retire, really. So we have a pretty good community of lifers in this prison. There are a few, a handful of guys, that are just always bummers all the time. You can't do nothing for them. They're far and few between."

26. According to Nigel Walker, "The original meaning of retribution was 'paying back' a literal debt or tax. In the philosophy of punishment there is no doubt that the retributive justification for a penalty is linked to what a person has done, not what he will do." Nigel Walker, *Why Punish?* (Oxford: Oxford University Press, 1991), p. 69.

27. A much-publicized analysis by Robert Martinson cast doubt on the degree to which rehabilitation programs worked effectively. The analysis was widely summarized by a slogan—"Nothing works"—that gained much public currency. Robert Martinson, "What Works— Questions and Answers about Prison Reform," *National Affairs* 1 (1974):

22–54. Martinson was hardly alone. See also Seymour Halleck and Ann Witte, "Is Rehabilitation Dead?" *Crime & Delinquency* 2 (1977): 372–383; Michael Serrill, "Is Rehabilitation Dead?" *Corrections Magazine* 1 (1975): 21–32. That Martinson's critique was flawed did not escape some contemporary analysts' attention (see Ted Palmer, *Correctional Intervention and Research: Current Issues and Future Prospects* [Lexington, MA: Lexington Books, 1978]), but it became part of the "common sense" of much criminological and political thought for a lengthy period of time. See Francis Cullen, "The Twelve People Who Saved Rehabilitation," *Criminology* 43 (2005): 1–42.

28. See American Friends Service Committee, *Struggle for Justice: A Report on Crime and Punishment in America* (New York: Hill and Wang, 1971).

29. On the rise of retribution, see Russell Christopher, "Deterring Retributivism: The Injustice of 'Just' Punishment," *Northwestern University Law Review* 96 (2002): 843–976; Robert Ferguson, *Inferno: An Anatomy of American Punishment* (Cambridge, MA: Harvard University Press, 2014); Brian Slattery, "The Myth of Retributive Justice," in *Retributivism and Its Critics,* ed. Wesley Craig (Stuttgart, Ger.: Franz Steiner Verlag, 1992), pp. 27–34.

30. As Nigel Walker notes, retribution "promises the certainty which utilitarianism cannot. The punisher can be sure that whatever else he may or may not be achieving, he is at least inflicting more or less what the offender deserves." Walker, *Why Punish?* p. 67.

31. Understood as a variant on vengeance, retribution dates to the earliest formulations of justice. See Meghan Ryan, "Proximate Retribution," *Houston Law Review* 48 (2012): 1049–1106. Of course, retribution is not the same as vengeance, at least in theory. Retribution differs from vengeance because it is meant to be directed only at criminal wrongs, should possess inherent limits, should not be personal, should involve no pleasure at suffering, and should follow procedural standards. See Robert Nozick, *Philosophical Investigations* (Cambridge, MA: Harvard University Press, 1981). As many commentators note, even during the heyday of rehabilitation, retribution remained a potent force in discussions of punishment in the United States. See Michele Cotton, "Back with a Vengeance: The Resilience of Retribution as an

Articulated Purpose of Criminal Punishment," *American Criminal Law Review* 37 (2000): 1313–1362; Ferguson, *Inferno;* Walker, *Why Punish?* Walker's observation here is a trenchant one: "The utilitarian tradition has had to contend with an even older one. The Greek philosophers were rationalists, but Greek mythology was full of vengeance" (p. 7).

32. See Steven Gey, "Justice Scalia's Death Penalty," *Florida State University Law Review* 20 (1992): 67–132; Walker, *Why Punish?* Part of the issue here is the difficulty in isolating the precise nature of the harm that retribution seeks to address. See Russ Shafer-Landau, "Retributivism and Desert," *Pacific Philosophical Quarterly* 81 (2000): 189–214; Slattery, "The Myth of Retributive Justice."

33. On the tendency of retributionist impulses to lead to ever-longer sentences, and on the general elasticity of the concept of retribution, see Julian Lamont, "The Concept of Desert in Distributive Justice," *Philosophical Quarterly* 44 (1994): 45–64; Alice Ristroph, "Desert, Democracy and Sentencing Reform," *Journal of Criminal Law and Criminology* 96 (2006): 1293–1352. Robert Ferguson puts the point forcefully: "The facts are these: a need to punish moves rather quickly into a desire to punish, habit reinforces that desire, severity has its own momentum in punishment regimes, and these regimes deteriorate over time through the imposition of greater levels of punishment than originally intended." Ferguson, *Inferno,* p. 59.

34. As Ristroph notes, "The notion of deserved punishment is deeply engrained in the way most people think and talk about the criminal law. Desert rhetoric is probably inescapable." Ristroph, "Desert, Democracy and Sentencing Reform," p. 1337. On the pervasiveness of retribution in everyday consciousness, see John Darley, "Citizens' Assignments of Punishments for Moral Transgressions: A Case Study in the Psychology of Punishment," *Ohio State Journal of Criminal Law* 8 (2010): 101–117. On the general moral sense that wrongdoing deserves punishment, see John Kleinig, *Punishment and Desert* (The Hague: Martinus Nijhoff, 1973); John Rawls, "Two Concepts of Rules," *Philosophical Review* 64 (1955): 3–32. Rawls summarizes the retributionist sentiment well: "It is morally fitting that a person who does wrong should suffer in proportion to his wrongdoing. That a criminal should be punished follows from his guilt, and the severity of the

appropriate punishment depends on the depravity of his act. The state of affairs where a wrongdoer suffers punishment is morally better than the state of affairs where he does not" (p. 4).

35. John Mackie, "Morality and the Retributive Emotions," *Criminal Justice Ethics* 1 (1982): 3–9.

36. Jean Hampton, a noted advocate of retribution, makes this point: "To say that [retribution] is a moral obligation, is not to say that it is an obligation that always prevails in a situation: there may be times when morality calls for mercy rather than punishment. In such a situation, mercy and justice conflict, and the moral obligation to be merciful trumps the moral obligation to inflict punishment. If one believes that one can have an obligation to be merciful, one cannot say that retributive punishment is always morally *required*." Jean Hampton, "An Expressive Theory of Retribution," in *Retributivism and Its Critics,* ed. Wesley Craig (Stuttgart, Ger.: Franz Steiner Verlag, 1992), pp. 1–25 (emphasis in original).

37. On punishment's moral lesson, see Herbert Morris, "Persons and Punishment," *The Monist* 52 (1968): 475–501. On the need to restore the value of a victim of crime, see Jean Hampton, "Correcting Harms versus Righting Wrongs: The Goal of Retribution," *UCLA Law Review* 39 (1992): 1659–1702. On the imperative to reinforce the collective consciousness of society, see Emile Durkheim, *The Division of Labor in Society* (New York: Macmillan, 1984).

38. R. Anthony Duff, *Punishment, Communication, and Community* (Oxford: Oxford University Press, 2003).

39. For this reason, it is unproductive to isolate a preferred approach to punishment as either retributionist or utilitarian. In reality, any punishment is likely to draw justifications from multiple philosophies. This is both sensible and in accord with public opinion. See Richard Frase, "Punishment Purposes," *Stanford Law Review* 58 (2005): 67–83; Walker, *Why Punish?* Further, as Ristroph notes, such an amalgamation of philosophies is an inherent part of any actual punishment regime. Ristroph, "Desert, Democracy and Sentencing Reform."

40. On the value of centering atonement in a philosophy of punishment, see Stephen P. Garvey, "Punishment as Atonement," *UCLA Law Review* 46 (1999): 1801–1858.

41. As Duff insightfully notes, this view of punishment usefully acknowledges both the need for punishment and the possibility of change, in a fashion that values both retributivist and consequentialist aims: "Punishment will now look both back (as retributivists insist it must) to a past crime as that which merits this response, and forward (as consequentialists insist it must) to some future good that it aims to achieve." Duff, *Punishment, Communication, and Community*, p. 89.

1. BECOMING EASY

1. A "write-up" is an occasion when a prisoner is cited by staff for violating a prison regulation. "The hole" is a prison colloquialism for solitary confinement.

2. Useful overviews of this literature include John Laub and Robert Sampson, "Understanding Desistance from Crime," *Crime and Justice* 28 (2001): 1–69; Michael Ezell and Lawrence Cohen, *Desisting from Crime* (Oxford: Oxford University Press, 2005); Lila Kazemian, "Desistance from Crime: Theoretical, Empirical, Methodological and Policy Considerations," *Journal of Contemporary Criminal Justice* 23 (2007): 5–27; Shadd Maruna and Heith Copes, "What Have We Learned from Five Decades of Neutralization Research?" *Crime and Justice* 32 (2005): 221–320.

3. See most notably Shadd Maruna, *Making Good: How Ex-convicts Reform and Rebuild Their Lives* (Washington, DC: American Psychological Association, 2001). See also Catherine Appleton, *Life after Life Imprisonment* (Oxford: Oxford University Press, 2010); Andreas Aresti, Virginia Eatough, and Belinda Brooks-Gordon, "Doing Time after Time: An Interpretative Phenomenological Analysis of Reformed Ex-prisoners' Experiences of Self-Change, Identity and Career Opportunities," *Psychology, Crime & Law* 16 (2010): 169–190; Lois Presser, "Violent Offenders, Moral Selves: Constructing Identities and Accounts in the Research Interview," *Social Problems* 51 (2004): 82–101; Neal Shover, *Great Pretenders: Pursuits and Careers of Persistent Thieves* (Oxford, U.K.: Westview Press, 1996); Barry Vaughn, "The Internal Narrative of Desistance," *British Journal of Criminology* 47 (2007): 390–404.

4. There is an academic debate about the role of self-narrative in the process of change. The pathbreaking work of Maruna (2001) suggests that, for convicted criminals, the construction of a new understanding of oneself is critical to the process of desisting from future crime. His data suggest a process through which criminals come to see their past offending as a temporary fall from grace and then reorient themselves toward recapturing their truer and better selves (see also Peggy Giordano, Stephen Cernkovich, and Jennifer Rudolph, "Gender, Crime, and Desistance: Toward a Theory of Cognitive Transformation," *American Journal of Sociology* 107 [2002]: 990–1064). Commonly, this subjective reorientation is reinforced through various projects of redemption, ones frequently focused on counseling other prisoners.

Of course, such individualistic accounts of prisoner change can be criticized for neglecting the various social factors that condition all human behavior, not least criminal behavior. From this perspective, desistance from crime cannot be understood solely as an individual choice, but must be regarded also as a behavioral dynamic importantly shaped by contextual factors (see John Laub and Ralph Sampson, *Shared Beginnings, Divergent Lives: Delinquent Boys to Age 70* (Cambridge, MA: Harvard University Press, 2003). As Vaughn ("The Internal Narrative of Desistance") notes, this issue can be recast as another version of the structure-agency debate—or as Thomas LeBel and his coauthors suggest, another version of the chicken-egg debate. Thomas LeBel, Ros Burnett, Shadd Maruna, and Shawn Bushway, "The 'Chicken and Egg' of Subjective and Social Factors in Desistance from Crime," *European Journal of Criminology* 5 (2008): 131–159.

The easiest answer here is likely the correct one—that individual agency is critical, but that it will emerge most strongly in social environments that encourage its flourishing. My data seem to confirm this. Many of those whom I interviewed were able to explain their desistance from crime as a component of a larger personal transformation. Yet those prisoners who had secure family relations and ongoing projects within the prison, such as work and education, told somewhat more compelling narratives of growth and change. So, my data appear to support the conclusion that reconstructed self-narratives are critical to maturation, but that social factors strongly influence the extent to which such narratives are accompanied by sturdy behavioral change. For an especially expansive and nuanced discussion of the various factors that contribute to desistance, see Laura Abrams and Diane Terry, *Everyday Desistance: The Transition to Adulthood among Formerly Incarcerated Youth* (New Brunswick, NJ: Rutgers University Press, 2017).

5. There is evidence that ex-offenders who actively seek to counsel others see growth in their levels of self-esteem and are better able to resist the negative impacts of the stigma associated with a conviction. See Thomas LeBel, Matt Richie, and Shadd Maruna, "Helping Others as a Response to Reconcile a Criminal Past: The Role of the Wounded Healer in Prisoner Reentry Programs," *Criminal Justice and Behavior* 42 (2015): 108–120. See also Bruce Arrigo and Yoshiko Takahashi, "Recommunalization of the Disenfranchised: A Theoretical and Criminological Inquiry," *Theoretical Criminology* 10 (2006): 307–336; J. David Brown, "The Professional Ex-: An Alternative for Exiting the Deviant Career," *Sociological Quarterly* 32 (1991): 219–230; Thomas LeBel, "An Examination of the Impact of Formerly Incarcerated Persons Helping Others," *Journal of Offender Rehabilitation* 26 (2007): 1–24; William White, "The History of Recovered People as Wounded Healers: The Era of Professionalization and Specialization," *Alcoholism Treatment Quarterly* 18 (2000): 1–25.

6. The range of works whose findings I replicate is wide and stretches across decades of research. See Timothy Flanagan, "Dealing with Long-Term Confinement: Adaptive Strategies and Perspectives among Long-Term Prisoners," *Criminal Justice and Behavior* 8 (1981): 201–222; John Irwin, *Lifers: Seeking Redemption in Prison* (New York: Routledge, 2009); Robert Johnson, *Hard Time: Understanding and Reforming the Prison* (Belmont, CA: Wadsworth, 2002); Robert Johnson and Ania Dobrzanska, "Mature Coping among Life-Sentenced Inmates: An Exploratory Study of Adjustment Dynamics," *Corrections Compendium* 30 (2005): 8–13; Margaret Leigey, *The Forgotten Men: Serving a Life without Parole Sentence* (New Brunswick, NJ: Rutgers University Press, 2015); Wilfried Rasch, "The Effects of Indeterminate Detention: A Study of Men Sentenced to Life Imprisonment," *International Journal of Law and Psychiatry* 4 (1981): 417–431; Edward Zamble, "Behavior and

Adaptation in Long-Term Prison Inmates: Descriptive Longitudinal Results," *Criminal Justice and Behavior* 12 (1992): 409–425.

7. On the role of lifers in providing stability inside prisons, see James Paluch, *A Life for a Life* (Oxford: Oxford University Press, 2003).

8. I do not wish to suggest that the lifers I interviewed are by any means representative of the lifer population as a whole. Indeed, there is much evidence that many life-sentenced prisoners do not cope nearly as well with their sentences as the ones I interviewed. On the struggles that many life-sentenced prisoners face, and the inability of many to cope effectively, see Marguerite Schinkel, *Being Imprisoned: Adaptation and Desistance* (London: Palgrave, 2014). However, even if I can make only limited claims regarding the representativeness of my sample, the consistencies across my interviews were striking. And, as noted, my findings accord with a range of other interview-based studies of lifers. Easy keepers are thus a group of life-sentenced prisoners that is large enough to be a worthy subject of study and a deserving target of reconstructed sentencing policy.

9. The change that life-sentenced prisoners exhibit may be due in significant part to their simple acculturation to life in prison. In that sense, the ability to adjust well to prison life may not foretell successful adaptation to life outside of prison. This may mean that a new self-narrative is not sufficient, in and of itself, to ensure that a long-term prisoner will succeed if released. On this point, see Craig Haney, "The Psychological Impact of Incarceration: Implications for Postprison Adjustment," in *Prisoners Once Removed: The Impact of Incarceration on Children, Families and Communities,* ed. Jeremy Travis and Michelle Waul (Washington, DC: Urban Institute, 2003), pp. 33–66; Susie Hulley, Ben Crewe, and Serena Wright, "Re-examining the Problems of Long-Term Imprisonment," *British Journal of Criminology* 56 (2016): 769–792; Marieke Liem, *After Life Imprisonment: Reentry in the Era of Mass Incarceration* (New York: NYU Press, 2016). That said, recidivism rates for older ex-offenders are generally low, especially for those convicted of murder, and the rates of infractions that prisoners commit generally decline with age. See Mark Cunningham and James Sorenson, "Nothing to Lose? A Comparative Examination of Prison Misconduct Rates

among Life-without-Parole and Other Long-Term High-Security Inmates," *Criminal Justice and Behavior* 33 (2006): 683–705; James Sorenson and Jonathan Marquart, "Future Dangerousness and Incapacitation," in *American's Experiment with Capital Punishment: Reflections on the Past, Present and Future of the Ultimate Penal Sanction,* ed. James Acker, Robert Bohm, and Charles Lanier (Durham, NC: Carolina Academic Press, 2003), pp. 283–300; James Sorenson and Robert Wrinkle, "No Hope for Parole: Disciplinary Infractions among Death-Sentenced and Life-without-Parole Inmates," *Criminal Justice and Behavior* 23 (1996): 542–552; Hans Toch and Kenneth Adams, *Acting Out: Maladaptive Behavior in Confinement* (Washington, DC: American Psychological Association, 2002). If survival in prison requires behavioral changes that inhibit successful resocialization after release, the best way forward is to reduce sentence lengths and to increase the availability of opportunities for prisoners to engage in constructive activities and social relations while inside.

10. On the use of violence to maintain or enhance one's status in prison, see Rebecca Trammell, *Enforcing the Convict Code: Violence and Prison Culture* (Boulder, CO: Lynne Rienner, 2012).

11. It might not be a coincidence that Leonard and Rudy came to their new orientation to life in their midtwenties. Current brain science indicates that, for men especially, full development of the brain continues well into the twenties. See Elkhonon Goldberg, *The Executive Brain: Frontal Lobes and the Civilized Mind* (Oxford: Oxford University Press, 2001); Sara Johnson, Robert Blum, and Jay Giedd, "Adolescent Maturity and the Brain: The Promise and Pitfalls of Neuroscience Research in Adolescent Health Policy," *Journal of Adolescent Health* 45 (2009): 216–221. On the issue of whether newer understandings of brain development should shape justice policy, see Laurence Steinberg, "Should the Science of Adolescent Brain Development Inform Public Policy?" *American Psychologist* 64 (2009): 739–750.

12. On the initial struggles of individuals to adapt to a long-term prison sentence, see Roger Sapsford, *Life Sentence Prisoners: Reaction, Response and Change* (London: Open University Press, 1983).

13. Irwin, *Lifers,* p. 66, emphasis in original. See also Liem, *After Life Imprisonment.*

14. See also Leigey, *Forgotten Men.*

15. On the importance of mentoring to life-sentenced prisoners, see also ibid.; Hans Toch, "'I Am Not Now Who I Used to Be Then': Risk Assessment and the Maturation of Long-Term Prison Inmates," *Prison Journal* 90 (2010): 4–11.

16. On the role of preexisting trauma in helping explain the types of violence that provoke individuals to earn long-term sentences, see James Garabino, *Listening to Killers: Lessons Learned from My Twenty Years as a Psychological Expert Witness in Murder Cases* (Oakland: University of California Press, 2015). On the overall prevalence of trauma in the histories of prisoners, see Tina Maschi, Sandy Gibson, Kristen Zgoba, and Keith Morgen, "Trauma and Life Event Stressors among Young and Older Adult Prisoners," *Journal of Correctional Health Care* 17 (2011): 160–172.

17. White, "The History of Recovered People." See also LeBel, Ritchie, and Maruna, "Helping Others as a Response"; Shadd Maruna, Thomas LeBel, and Charles Lanier, "Generativity behind Bars: Some 'Redemptive Truth' about Prison Society," in *The Generative Society: Caring for Future Generations,* ed. Ed St. Aubin, Dan McAdams, and Tae-Chang Kim (Washington, DC: American Psychological Association, 2004), pp. 131–151; Toch, "I Am Not Now."

18. Maruna, *Making Good.*

19. Ben Crewe, Susie Hulley, and Serena Wright capture the general orientation of many long-term prisoners well in an analysis of the extensive interviews they conducted: "Participants who were further into their sentences had generally come to accept their predicament, worked out which areas of their lives they could and could not control, and begun to find purpose and meaning in their lives. Their focus was less on the past than the future, and their use of the present was constructive rather than merely depletive. Despite—and in some ways because of—their overarching stoicism with regard to their general circumstances, in their daily practices, they exhibited a form of productive agency, in which they sought to make the most of a situation that was not of their choosing, but from which they believed they could derive some personal value. Within the prison's structural cocoon, then, they were agentically active." Ben Crewe, Susie Hulley,

and Serena Wright, "Swimming with the Tide: Adapting to Long-Term Imprisonment," *Justice Quarterly* 34 (2017): 517–541.

20. On the necessity of hope for prisoners seeking to maintain a changed self-narrative, see Leigey *Forgotten Men;* Maruna, *Making Good.*

21. Of course, the limited horizons of the futures that lifers can imagine is a notable constraint against which they must struggle. On this point, see Crewe, Hulley, and Wright, "Swimming with the Tide."

22. Appleton, in her interview-based study of prisoners who earned long sentences, noted that her research subjects saw death in prison as "the ultimate failure." Appleton, *Life after Life Imprisonment,* p. 151.

23. In his study of prisoners sentenced to life imprisonment, Rasch reached this conclusion: "The results suggest the existence of a seemingly infinite human capacity to cope with the stress of an inhumane condition—long-term imprisonment." Rasch, "The Effects of Indeterminate Detention," p. 430.

2. BEING EASY ISN'T EASY

1. The classic text on the pains of punishment is Gresham Sykes, *The Society of Captives: A Study of a Maximum Security Prison* (Princeton, NJ: Princeton University Press, 1958). Additional works along these lines include Ben Crewe, "Depth, Weight, Tightness: Revisiting the Pains of Imprisonment," *Punishment and Society* 13 (2011): 509–529; Benjamin Fleury-Steiner and Jamie Longazel, *The Pains of Mass Imprisonment* (New York: Routledge, 2013); Robert Johnson, *Hard Time: Understanding and Reforming the Prison* (Belmont, CA: Wadsworth, 2001); Lori Sexton, "Penal Subjectivities: Developing a Theoretical Framework for Penal Consciousness," *Punishment and Society* 17 (2015): 114–136; Hans Toch, *Living in Prison: The Ecology of Survival* (New York: Free Press, 1977); Hans Toch and Kenneth Adams, *Acting Out: Maladaptive Behavior in Confinement* (Washington, DC: American Psychological Association, 2002). For an analysis of the more specific pains of imprisonment that beset life-sentenced prisoners, see Margaret Leigey and Michael Ryder, "The Pains of Permanent Imprisonment: Examining Perceptions of Confinement among Older Life without Parole

Inmates," *International Journal of Offender Therapy and Comparative Criminology* 59 (2015): 726–742. For first-person accounts of inmates' struggles under a life sentence, see Erin George, *A Woman Doing Life: Notes from a Prison for Women* (Oxford: Oxford University Press, 2010); Victor Hassine, *Life without Parole: Living and Dying in Prison Today* (Oxford: Oxford University Press, 2010); James Paluch, *A Life for a Life* (Oxford: Oxford University Press, 2003).

Some authors make a stronger argument: that prisons work to actively harm their occupants. In other words, it is not just that inmates suffer pains but that prison life works to degrade them. See Todd Clear, *Harm in American Penology: Offenders, Victims and Their Communities* (Albany: State University of New York Press, 1994); John Irwin, *The Warehouse Prison: Disposal of the New Dangerous Class* (Los Angeles: Roxbury, 2005).

For her part, Elaine Crawley mobilizes the term *thoughtlessness* to describe much treatment of inmates, particularly those who are aging. Such thoughtlessness includes, for Crawley, an unwillingness to ensure that aged prisoners can have a bottom bunk bed. Elaine Crawley, "Institutional Thoughtlessness in Prisons and Its Impacts on the Day-to-Day Prison Lives of Elderly Men," *Journal of Contemporary Criminal Justice* 21 (2005): 350–363. On this, see also Margaret Leigey, *The Forgotten Men: Serving a Life without Parole Sentence* (New Brunswick, NJ: Rutgers University Press, 2015).

Whether *pain, harm,* or *thoughtlessness* best characterizes one or another component of prison life is a difficult question to arbitrate, largely because institutions differ so significantly. It is likely that the aptness of one term versus the other varies from one prison experience to another.

2. This emphasis on degradation runs throughout the criminal process. See the classic text by Harold Garfinkel, "Conditions of Successful Degradation Ceremonies," *American Journal of Sociology* 61 (1956): 420–424. Another important sociological tradition that emphasizes the symbolic components of punishment derives from the seminal work of Emile Durkheim. For Durkheim, the social processes of designating and punishing criminals were functional to the creation of social order. The criminal process enables society to demarcate

between good and evil, between sacred and profane. These distinctions, Durkheim argued, reinforced the underlying moral order that is crucial to social order more generally. See Emile Durkheim, *The Division of Labor in Society* (New York: Macmillan, 1984). For classic analyses that emphasize the good/evil and sacred/profane binaries, see Mary Douglas, *Purity and Danger: An Analysis of Concepts of Pollution and Taboo* (London: Routledge, 2002); Kai Erickson, *Wayward Puritans: A Study in the Sociology of Deviance* (Boston: Allyn & Bacon, 2004).

For a more recent Durkheimian analysis of the culture of punishment, see Philip Smith, *Culture and Punishment* (Chicago: University of Chicago Press, 2008). Other useful, and more critical, analyses of the Durkheimian approach to punishment can be found in David Garland, *Punishment and Modern Society: A Study in Social Theory*. Chicago: University of Chicago Press, 1990); Joshua Page, "Eliminating the Enemy: The Import of Denying Prisoners' Access to Higher Education in Clinton's America," *Punishment & Society* 6 (2004): 357–378. The ability of easy keepers to retain a strong sense of connection to the various social groups of which they are a part is all the more remarkable given the symbolic barriers that punishment erects against them. I develop this line of analysis further in Steve Herbert, "Inside or Outside? Expanding the Narratives about Life-Sentenced Prisoners," *Punishment and Society,* forthcoming.

3. Irwin argues that staff symbolically denigrate prisoners to obviate their guilt for enforcing rules that so clearly inflict harm. This may well be true, but it is hard to know which comes first—the symbolic castigation or the material deprivation. Perhaps it is best to recognize that they are yoked together, and that ameliorating one will require addressing the other. Certainly, any effort to address the material conditions facing life-sentenced prisoners will necessitate addressing the symbolic politics of punishment. John Irwin, *Lifers: Seeking Redemption in Prison* (New York: Routledge, 2009).

4. Eamonn Carrabine notes that the power of routines rests in part on the symbolic message they convey. As he puts it, routines represent "the dull compulsion of rituals that powerfully constrain action and signify the inevitability of the social structure." Eamonn Carrabine, "Prison Riots, Social Order and the Problem of Legitimacy," *British Journal of Criminology* 45 (2005): 904.

5. COs are custody officers.

6. Richard Sparks, Anthony Bottoms, and Will Hay argue that prisons run better when inmates can understand the logic of regulations. They suggest that prisoners are more likely to comply with rules that can be legitimated with norms that are broadly recognized as fair. Richard Sparks, Anthony Bottoms, and Will Hay, *Prisons and the Problem of Order* (Oxford, U.K.: Clarendon Press, 1996). This line of analysis is supported by the work on procedural justice done by Tom Tyler. For Tyler, compliance with the law is more readily forthcoming from citizens who can understand the logic behind any law that might be enforced against them. See especially Tom Tyler, *Why People Obey the Law: Procedural Justice, Legitimacy and Compliance* (New Haven, CT: Yale University Press, 1990); Tom Tyler and Yuen Huo, *Trust in the law: Encouraging Public Cooperation with the Police and Courts* (New York: Russell Sage Foundation, 2002).

7. A kite is a written communication between a prisoner and a member of the prison staff, usually a counselor.

8. A substantial body of literature supports Melvin's stress on the importance of respectful treatment on the part of prison staff. These works suggest that prisons run more smoothly when such respect is reinforced in daily interactions between staff and inmates. See Johnson, *Hard Time*; Alison Liebling, *Prisons and Their Moral Performance: A Study of Values, Quality, and Prison Life* (Oxford: Oxford University Press, 2004); Sparks, Bottoms, and Hay, *Prisons and the Problem of Order*; Kevin N. Wright and Laura Bronstein, "Creating Decent Prisons," *Journal of Offender Rehabilitation* 44 (2007): 1–16. In addition, Marguerite Schinkel argues that prisoners are more likely to engage in projects of self-change if they believe that their individuality is recognized and respected. Marguerite Schinkel, *Being Imprisoned: Punishment, Adaptation and Desistance* (London: Palgrave, 2014). Craig Haney puts the matter clearly: "The quality of prison life and the nature of correctional treatment can compound or alleviate the vulnerabilities with which persons enter prison. This means that prisoners who are confined in safe and caring facilities, and who experience fair treatment during incarceration, experience a greater sense of well-being and are less likely to experience negative outcomes during incarceration." Craig Haney,

Reforming Punishment: Psychological Limits to the Pains of Imprisonment (Washington, DC: American Psychological Association, 2009), p. 225.

9. For a review of the array of monetary sanctions that can accompany a criminal conviction, see Alexes Harris, Beth Huebner, Karin Martin, Mary Pattillo, Becky Pettit, Sarah Shannon, Bryan Sykes, Chris Uggen, and April Fernandes, *Monetary Sanctions in the Criminal Justice System* (Houston: John and Laura Arnold Foundation, 2017); Alexes Harris, Heather Evans, and Katherine Beckett, "Drawing Blood from Stones: Legal Debt and Social Inequality in the Contemporary United States." *American Journal of Sociology* 115 (2010): 1753–1799.

10. Jobs that helped with the administration of the prison—such as serving food, doing laundry, and performing cleaning duties—paid $.42 an hour at the time of the interviews. The most coveted jobs were with Correctional Industries, but these paid only $1.40 an hour. Correctional Industries is a component of the Department of Corrections and employs prisoners to produce a range of goods for various state agencies.

11. Irwin makes a particularly strong version of this argument: "The outcome of new employees' inculcation with the existing informal guard culture and their interactions with prisoners—most of whom hate the guards and many of whom attempt to manipulate them to increase their levels of privilege and material means—results in guards and staff distrusting, demeaning, and often hating prisoners." Irwin, *Lifers*, p. 65. Kauffman makes a similar argument with respect to prison officers' justification of the violence they sometimes meted out: "Regardless of their own moral inhibitions regarding violence, substantial numbers of officers eventually came to use it against inmates. They sought to neutralize their guilt over violating moral laws to which they subscribed by postulating that the prison world constituted a separate moral realm or that inmates were beings beyond the embrace of moral laws." Kelsey Kauffman, *Prison Officers and Their World* (Cambridge, MA: Harvard University Press, 1988), p. 229. Joshua Page notes that this moral denigration of prisoners has political benefits, as well. In his account of the rise of the political power of correctional officers' labor unions in California, he notes the importance of the symbolic denigration of prisoners. Guards sought to mobilize pub-

lic sympathy by emphasizing the dangers that they were assuming by overseeing morally tainted criminals. Joshua Page, *The Toughest Beat: Politics, Punishment and the Prison Officers Union in California* (New York: Oxford University Press, 2011).

12. On the struggles lifers experience in maintaining familial relations, see Yvonne Jewkes, "Loss, Liminality and the Life Sentence: Managing Identify through a Disrupted Lifecourse," in *The Effects of Imprisonment*, edited by Alison Liebling and Shadd Maruna (Portland, OR: Willan, 2005), pp. 366–388.

13. Kerbs and Jolley note that, as prisoners age, their concern for a quiet, secure, hassle-free existence can understandably motivate them to withdraw from prison life. This is one of the realities that underlies arguments for institutions more explicitly designed for elderly prisoners. John Kerbs and Jennifer Jolley, "A Commentary on Age Segregation for Older Prisoners: Philosophical and Pragmatic Considerations," *Criminal Justice Review* 34 (2009): 119–132.

14. In the state of Washington, a close custody institution is the secondmost restrictive prison environment. The most restrictive environment is designated "intensive management," which is Washington's term for solitary confinement. Although life-sentenced prisoners must spend some time in a close custody institution for the first period of their confinement, they can earn a transfer to a medium-security institution if they compile a satisfactory behavioral record.

15. In his first-person account of his experience of a life sentence, Victor Hassine notes the pervasive presence of fear as a central component of daily life. Hassine, *Life without Parole*. See also Thomas Schmid and Richard Jones, "Suspended Identity: Identity Transformation in a Maximum Security Prison," *Symbolic Interaction* 14 (1991): 415–432.

16. On the norms of masculinity that pervade many prisons, see Tony Evans and Patti Wallace, "A Prison within a Prison? The Masculinity Narratives of Male Prisoners," *Men and Masculinities* 10 (2008): 484–507; Hans Toch, "Hypermasculinity and Prison Violence," in *Masculinities and Violence*, edited by Lee Bowker (Thousand Oaks, CA: Sage, 1998), pp. 168–178.

17. Craig Haney astutely notes that prisons operate in ways that defy the conventional wisdom of the field of psychology, most notably

the well-established relation between stress and human agency. As he notes, stress decreases with one's control over the immediate environment. Put differently, the vulnerability that most prisoners feel is a notable impediment to their psychological well-being. Craig Haney, *Reforming Punishment*.

18. On the importance of opportunities for lifers to engage with meaningful programs, see Jessica Henry, "Reducing Severe Sentences: The Role of Prison Programming in Sentencing Reform," *Criminology and Public Policy* 14 (2015): 397–405. Henry observes, "Prison programs that target [long-term prisoners] send a clear message to policy makers, society, and individual offenders that their personal growth matters, that their humanity is valued, and that their inherent dignity as a person is recognized. Prison programs afford transformational opportunities and allow an offender to be more than just a nameless inmate, waiting only until death to be released" (p. 400).

19. As I noted in the introduction, there is no necessary disjuncture between retribution and rehabilitation, a theme to which I return in chapter 4.

20. Charlie potentially could be released because he earned his life-without-parole sentence while a juvenile. A key U.S. Supreme Court case, *Miller v. Alabama*, ruled that mandatory life-without-parole sentences for juveniles were unconstitutional. A subsequent U.S. Supreme Court case, *Montgomery v. Louisiana*, required states to apply this ruling retroactively. For that reason, Charlie was eligible for resentencing, which could enable his eventual release from prison.

21. Unsurprisingly, prisoners express considerable fear of dying in prison. See Ronald Aday, "Aging Prisoners' Concerns toward Dying in Prison," *OMEGA: Journal of Death and Dying* 52 (2006): 199–216.

3. WHEN EASY BECOMES HARD

1. A classification counselor has a range of responsibilities, including ensuring that prisoners have opportunities to remain active. Each inmate is assigned a counselor and works with that individual to secure jobs or to participate in programs. The counselors are also

responsible for overseeing the process through which an inmate changes his custody status. This explains the term *classification* in the title, because these counselors can help move the inmate from one custody category to another.

2. Exceptions can be made for reformatory inmates in need of dialysis. The dialysis unit is located on the third floor. Inmates who need dialysis are typically housed on the third floor of their cell block to ease their ability to get to their treatments. If they are unable to use the stairs to get to the chow hall, their meals are delivered to the day room.

3. One staff member noted the unfortunate reality of the colloquial term *pusher,* used to designate a therapy aid. It seems, he noted, an inapt term in a prison where several inmates are housed for their role in the delivery of illegal drugs.

4. *Store* refers to the prison commissary, from which prisoners can purchase food and other goods.

5. *Mainline* specifically refers to meal time, when prisoners move to the chow hall to eat. It refers, more generally, to being part of the daily life of the prison. *Going to the mainline* refers to the capacity to conduct daily affairs alongside able-bodied prisoners.

6. Prisoners in Washington are assigned to one of four broad categories of prison: maximum, close, medium, or minimum. The higher the classification, the more restricted the environment. Lifers are rarely assigned to anything lower than medium security. Because the Sage Unit is in a minimum-security prison, lifers are almost never sent there.

7. On the value of programs and prisons tailored specifically for the elderly, see Mary Harrison, "True Grit: An Innovative Program for Elderly Inmates," *Corrections Today* 68 (2006): 46–49; Mary Harrison and Jim Benedetti, "Comprehensive Geriatric Programs in a Time of Shrinking Resources: 'True Grit' Revisited," *Corrections Today* 71 (2009): 44–47. For general overviews of the challenges that elderly prisoners pose to staff in facilities, see Ronald Aday, *Aging Prisoners: Crisis in American Corrections* (Westport, CT: Praeger, 2003); Tina Maschi, Mary Beth Morrissey, Russ Immarigeon, and Samantha Sutfin, *Aging Prisoners: A Crisis in Need of Intervention* (New York: Fordham Uni-

versity Be the Evidence Project, 2013); Glenda Reimer, "The Graying of the U.S. Prisoner Population," *Journal of Correctional Health Care* 14 (2008): 202–208. It is not simply that prisoners decline with age, but that the specific requirements of prison life, such as the common need to climb onto a top bunk or to drop to the floor if there is an alarm, are particularly difficult for the elderly. See Brie Williams, Karla Lindquist, Rebecca Sudore, Heidi Strupp, Donna Willmott, and Louise Walter, "Being Old and Doing Time: Functional Impairment and Adverse Experiences of Geriatric Female Prisoners," *Journal of the American Geriatrics Society* 54 (2006): 702–707.

8. Rikard and Rosenberg argue that prisoners are commonly physiologically ten years older than their counterparts outside. Robert Rikard and Ed Rosenberg, "Aging Inmates: A Convergence of Trends in the American Criminal Justice System," *Journal of Correctional Health Care* 13 (2007): 150–162. See also Seena Fazel, Tony Hope, Ian O'Donnell, Mary Piper, and Robin Jacoby, "Health of Elderly Male Prisoners: Worse Than the General Population, Worse Than Younger Prisoners," *Age and Ageing* 30 (2001): 403–407.

9. The provision of quality health care in prisons is no easy matter under the best of circumstances. Part of the problem is the lack of access to sufficient resources. Moreover, the priority that the DOC places on creating secure institutions can impede the delivery of health care, an issue that I address in chapter 4. On the general challenges of prison health care, especially for elderly prisoners, see Elaine Gallagher, "Elders in Prison: Health and Well-Being of Older Inmates," *International Journal of Law and Psychiatry* 24 (2001): 325–333; Susan Loeb and Azzu AbuDagga, "Health-Related Research on Older Inmates: An Integrative Literature Review," *Research in Nursing and Health* 29 (2006): 556–565; Roger Watson, Anne Stimpson, and Tony Hostick, "Prison Health Care: A Review of the Literature," *International Journal of Nursing Studies* 41 (2004): 119–128. For an account of how prisoners can experience a lack of quality health care, see Lori Sexton, "Penal Subjectivities: Developing a Theoretical Framework for Penal Consciousness," *Punishment and Society* 17 (2015): 114–136.

10. On the challenges that prisons face in dealing with the practical and ethical issues that accompany the increasing numbers of prisoners

with dementia, see Tina Maschi, Jung Kaw, Eunjeong Ko, and Mary Morrissey, "Forget Me Not: Dementia in Prison," *Gerontologist* 52 (2012): 441–451; John Wilson and Sharen Barboza, "The Looming Challenge of Dementia in Prisons," *Correct Care* 24 (2010): 10–13; Seena Fazel, John McMillan, and Ian O'Donnell, "Dementia in Prison: Ethical and Legal Implications," *Journal of Medical Ethics* 28 (2002): 156–159.

11. On the general challenges that prisons face in creating conditions for a comfortable death for terminally ill prisoners, see Ronald Aday and Azrini Wahidin, "Older Prisoners' Experiences of Death, Dying and Grief behind Bars," *Howard Journal of Crime and Justice* 55 (2016): 312–327; John Dawes, "Dying with Dignity: Prisoners and Terminal Illness," *Illness, Crisis, & Loss* 10 (2002): 188–203; Heath Hoffman and George Dickinson, "Characteristics of Prison Hospice Programs in the United States," *American Journal of Hospice and Palliative Medicine* 28 (2011): 245–252; Svetlana Yampolskaya and Norma Winston, "Hospice Care in Prison: General Principles and Outcomes," *American Journal of Hospice and Palliative Medicine* 20 (2003): 290–296.

12. According to prison staff, the reformatory did experiment with allowing an outside hospice organization provide end-of-life care to their dying prisoners. That arrangement did not work, the staff said, because the organization could not adapt to the limitations that a prison environment placed on the services they could offer.

4. LET'S ALL BE EASY

1. Not all states, of course, have eliminated the possibility that lifers can get out on parole. That said, many parole systems in the United States are helping detain prisoners for far longer terms than in the past. Parole systems are increasingly controlled by governors who are fearful of released prisoners committing crimes once outside, and are generally much more conservative than in past decades. See Nazgol Ghandnoosh, *Delaying a Second Chance: The Declining Prospects for Parole on Life Sentences* (Washington, DC: Sentencing Project, 2017).

2. Older prisoners rarely engage in prison misconduct, and they rarely return to prison when released. See Mark Cunningham and James Sorenson, "Nothing to Lose? A Comparative Examination of

Prison Misconduct Rates among Life-without-Parole and Other Long-Term High-Security inmates," *Criminal Justice and Behavior* 33 (2006): 683–705; James Sorenson and Jonathan Marquart, "Future Dangerousness and Incapacitation," in *American's Experiment with Capital Punishment: Reflections on the Past, Present and Future of the Ultimate Penal Sanction,* ed. James Acker, Robert Bohm, and Charles Lanier (Durham, NC: Carolina Academic Press, 2003), pp. 283–300; James Sorenson and Robert Wrinkle, "No Hope for Parole: Disciplinary Infractions among Death-Sentenced and Life-without-Parole Inmates," *Criminal Justice and Behavior* 23 (1996): 542–552; Hans Toch and Kenneth Adams, *Acting Out: Maladaptive Behavior in Confinement* (Washington, DC: American Psychological Association, 2002).

3. On the value of programming for life-sentenced prisoners, see Jessica Henry, "Reducing Severe Sentences: The Role of Prison Programming in Sentencing Reform," *Criminology and Public Policy* 14 (2015): 397–405; Rick Ruddell, Ian Broom, and Matthew Young, "Creating Hope for Life-Sentenced Prisoners," *Journal of Offender Rehabilitation* 49 (2010): 324–341.

4. Amy Lerman makes much the same point about the effects on prisoners when institutional practices send symbolic messages that emphasize their status as social pariahs: "By identifying inmates as 'offenders' and isolating them along with others defined by this negative valence, prisons may inadvertently create or reinforce an oppositional group identity." Amy Lerman, *The Modern Prison Paradox: Politics, Punishment, and Social Community* (Cambridge: Cambridge University Press, 2013), p. 58. Craig Haney makes a similar argument: "The degraded conditions under which prisoners live serve as constant reminders of their compromised and stigmatized social status and role. A diminished sense of self-worth and personal value may result." Craig Haney, *Reforming Punishment: Psychological Limits to the Pains of Imprisonment* (Washington, DC: American Psychological Association, 2009), p. 177.

5. Elaine Crawley writes sensitively about the felt need on the part of prison staff to remain emotionally detached from the inmates with which they work. See Elaine Crawley, "Emotion and Performance: Prison Officers and the Presentation of Self in Prisons," *Punishment and Society* 6 (2004): 411–427. Unfortunately, prisoners report that caring

relations are often critical to any efforts at successful personal change. See Catherine Appleton, *Life after Life Imprisonment* (Oxford: Oxford University Press, 2010).

6. For strong arguments concerning the capacity of custody concerns to trump the ability to provide effective medical care, see Elizabeth Alexander, "Cruel and Unusual Punishment: Litigating under the Eighth Amendment," *University of Pennsylvania Journal of Constitutional Law* 11 (2008–2009): 1–22; Benjamin Fleury-Steiner, *Dying Inside: The HIV/AIDS Ward at Limestone Prison* (Ann Arbor: University of Michigan Press, 2008); Michael Vaughn and Linda Smith, "Practicing Penal Harm Medicine in the United States: Prisoners' Voices from Jails," *Justice Quarterly* 16 (1999): 175–231.

7. An important issue here is the prisoner's ability to advocate for himself. Health research suggests that the greater a patient is actively engaged in self-efficacy, the better the health outcomes. In prison settings, such self-efficacy is possible but can be difficult to achieve, given the routine-driven and often oppressive nature of daily life. See Susan Loeb, Darrel Steffensmeier, and Cathy Kassab, "Predictors of Self-Efficacy and Self-Rated Health for Older Male Inmates," *Journal of Advanced Nursing* 67 (2011): 811–820.

8. For overviews of the issue of dementia in America's prison population and the ethical challenges that can result, see Tina Maschi, Jung Kaw, Eunjeong Ko, and Mary Morrissey, "Forget Me Not: Dementia in Prison," *Gerontologist* 52 (2012): 441–451; John Wilson and Sharen Barboza, "The Looming Challenge of Dementia in Prisons," *Correct Care* 24 (2010): 10–13; Seena Fazel, John McMillan, and Ian O'Donnell, "Dementia in Prison: Ethical and Legal Implications," *Journal of Medical Ethics* 28 (2002): 156–159.

9. *SOU* stands for Special Offenders Unit. It is a separate prison that houses individuals with mental illness.

10. Given their particular needs and vulnerabilities, elderly prisoners arguably deserve to spend their time behind bars in a setting that is tailored to their particular needs. See Ronald Aday, *Aging Prisoners: Crisis in American Corrections* (Westport, CT: Praeger, 2003); John Kerbs and Jennifer Jolley, "A Commentary on Age Segregation for Older Prisoners: Philosophical and Pragmatic Considerations for

Correctional Systems," *Criminal Justice Review* 34 (2009): 119–139; Robert Rikard and Ed Rosenberg, "Aging Inmates: A Convergence of Trends in the American Criminal Justice System," *Journal of Correctional Heßalth Care* 13 (2007): 150–162.

11. On the low rates of reoffending on the part of elderly convicts, both in prison and after release, see Osborne Association, *The High Costs of Low Risk: The Crisis of America's Aging Prison Population* (New York: Osborne Association, 2014). As that report puts it: "Despite the staggering costs of incarcerating the elderly—which far exceed any other correctional population—aging adults in prison have the lowest recidivism rate and pose almost no threat to public safety" (p. 5). See also Barry Mitchell and Julian Roberts, *Exploring the Mandatory Life Sentence for Murder* (Oxford, U.K.: Hart, 2012). Mitchell and Roberts argue that these low rates of reoffense contradict the common narrative of the essential predatory nature of those who commit murder and other violent crimes and, thus, contradict the legitimacy of the life sentence.

12. There is some dispute about just how many of those who previously committed homicide recidivate and, if they do so, whether the new crimes they commit are crimes of violence. The literature suggests that the rates of reoffense for a crime of violence are low. See Marieke Liem, "Homicide Offender Recidivism: A Review of the Literature," *Aggression and Violent Behavior* 18 (2013): 19–25; Marieke Liem, Margaret Zahn, and Lisa Tichavsky, "Criminal Recidivism among Homicide Offenders," *Journal of Interpersonal Violence* 29 (2014): 2630–2651.

13. As Craig Haney notes about the cultural currents that undergird America's steroid-laced punishment policy: "When punishment is justified through the demonization of those against whom it is directed, emphatic responses are thwarted. As a result, it has not been fashionable to discuss the suffering of people whom we have decided to punish harshly." Haney, *Reforming Punishment*, p. 9.

14. On the broad need to reconsider the increased number of life sentences in the United States, see Lila Kazemian and Jeremy Travis, "Imperative for Inclusion of Long Termers and Lifers in Research and Policy," *Criminology and Public Policy* 14 (2015): 355–395; Michael Tonry,

"Assessing the State of Mass Incarceration: Tipping Point or the New Normal?" *Criminology and Public Policy* 13 (2014): 567–577.

15. On the decreasing ability of parole systems to provide the shortened sentences that many prisoners deserve, see Ghandnoosh, *Delaying a Second Chance.*

16. As Martha Nussbaum notes, "The retributive attitude has a we/them mentality, in which judges set themselves above offenders, looking at their actions as if from a lofty height and preparing to find satisfaction in their pain." She argues that judges should adopt a more empathetic attitude toward those they sentence. A judge, she argues, "should remind himself at every turn that he himself is capable of the failings he reproves in others." Martha Nussbaum, "Equity and Mercy," *Philosophy & Public Affairs* 22 (1993): 103. Todd Clear puts the point more trenchantly: "To use the law as an instrument of repression erodes the law's moral force." Todd Clear, *Harm in American Penology: Offenders, Victims and Their Communities* (Albany: State University of New York Press, 1994), p. 32.

17. Such a policy would also work to temper the desire for vengeance that is rather too central to the culture and politics of American punishment. On the undercurrents of such vengeance, see Paul Kaplan, *Murder Stories: Ideological Narratives in Capital Punishment* (Lanham, MD: Lexington Books, 2012); Franklin Zimring, *The Contradictions of American Capital Punishment* (Oxford: Oxford University Press, 2003). What these less-rational impulses occlude is the capacity to see the inherent worth of the convicted criminal. As Eva Nilsen argues, "The case for treating a convicted person as a human being with innate dignity and value, and for seeing punishment as it is actually experienced, is rarely found in discourse about punishment." Eva Nilsen, "Decency, Dignity and Desert: Restoring Ideals of Humane Punishment to Constitutional Discourse," *UC Davis Law Review* 41 (2007–2008): 111–165. On the need to restore concepts like dignity to our discourse on punishment, see Jonathan Simon, *Mass Incarceration on Trial* (New York: New Press, 2016).

18. A noted retributionist, Herbert Morris, sees retribution and rehabilitation as fundamentally opposed, largely owing to the moral

status of the criminal offender. As he puts it, "[Punishment] is associated with resentment, for the guilty are those who have done what they had no right to do by failing to exercise restraint when they might have and where others have. Therapy is not a response to a person who is at fault." Herbert Morris, "Persons and Punishment," *The Monist* 52 (1968): 483. This sentiment, however, presumes that a criminal offender can only ever possess one status. In his view, one is either a resentment-deserving criminal or an emotionally troubled therapy recipient. This suggestion that any person has only one status is rarely true. Most every human occupies more than one status at a time, and most of us change from one status to another multiple times over a lifetime. It is thus nonsensical, as well as immoral, to advance such an appallingly one-dimensional view of humans.

19. On the increased costs that elderly inmates impose on prison systems, see Rikard and Rosenberg, "Aging Inmates."

References

Abrams, Laura, and Diane Terry. *Everyday Desistance: The Transition to Adulthood among Formerly Incarcerated Youth.* New Brunswick, NJ: Rutgers University Press, 2017.

Aday, Ronald. "Aging Prisoners' Concerns toward Dying in Prison." *OMEGA: Journal of Death and Dying* 52 (2006): 199–216.

———. *Aging Prisoners: Crisis in American Corrections.* Westport, CT: Praeger, 2003.

Aday, Ronald, and Azrini Wahidin. "Older Prisoners' Experiences of Death, Dying and Grief behind Bars." *Howard Journal of Crime and Justice* 55 (2016): 312–327.

Alexander, Elizabeth. "Cruel and Unusual Punishment: Litigating under the Eighth Amendment." *University of Pennsylvania Journal of Constitutional Law* 11 (2008–2009): 1–22.

American Civil Liberties Union. *At America's Expense: The Mass Incarceration of the Elderly.* Washington, DC: ACLU, 2012.

American Friends Service Committee. *Struggle for Justice: A Report on Crime and Punishment in America.* New York: Hill and Wang, 1971.

Appleton, Catherine. *Life after Life Imprisonment.* Oxford: Oxford University Press, 2010.

Appleton, Catherine, and Bent Grover. "The Pros and Cons of Life Imprisonment." *British Journal of Criminology* 47 (2007): 597–615.

Aresti, Andreas, Virginia Eatough, and Belinda Brooks-Gordon. "Doing Time after Time: An Interpretative Phenomenological Analysis of Reformed Ex-prisoners' Experiences of Self-Change, Identity and Career Opportunities." *Psychology, Crime & Law* 16 (2010): 169–190.

Arrigo, Bruce, and Yoshiko Takahashi. "Recommunalization of the Disenfranchised: A Theoretical and Criminological Inquiry." *Theoretical Criminology* 10 (2006): 307–336.

Auerhaun, Kathleen. "Selective Incapacitation, Three Strikes, and the Problem of Aging Prison Populations: Using Simulation Modeling to See the Future." *Criminology and Public Policy* 1 (2002): 353–388.

Beckett, Katherine. *Making Crime Pay: Law and Order in Contemporary American Politics.* Oxford: Oxford University Press, 1997.

Brown, J. David. "The Professional Ex-: An Alternative for Exiting the Deviant Career." *Sociological Quarterly* 32 (1991): 219–230.

Carrabine, Eamonn. "Prison Riots, Social Order and the Problem of Legitimacy." *British Journal of Criminology* 45 (2005): 896–913.

Christopher, Russell. "Deterring Retributivism: The Injustice of 'Just' Punishment." *Northwestern University Law Review* 96 (2002): 843–976.

Clear, Todd. *Harm in American Penology: Offenders, Victims and Their Communities.* Albany: State University of New York Press, 1994.

Cotton, Michele. "Back with a Vengeance: The Resilience of Retribution as an Articulated Purpose of Criminal Punishment." *American Criminal Law Review* 37 (2000): 1313–1362.

Crawley, Elaine. "Emotion and Performance: Prison Officers and the Presentation of Self in Prisons." *Punishment and Society* 6 (2004): 411–427.

———. "Institutional Thoughtlessness in Prisons and Its Impacts on the Day-to-Day Prison Lives of Elderly Men." *Journal of Contemporary Criminal Justice* 21 (2005): 350–363.

Crewe, Ben. "Depth, Weight, Tightness: Revisiting the Pains of Imprisonment." *Punishment and Society* 13 (2011): 509–529.

Crewe, Ben, Susie Hulley, and Serena Wright. "Swimming with the Tide: Adapting to Long-Term Imprisonment." *Justice Quarterly* 34 (2017): 517–541.

Cullen, Francis. "The Twelve People Who Saved Rehabilitation." *Criminology* 43 (2005): 1–42.

Cunningham, Mark, and James Sorenson. "Nothing to Lose? A Comparative Examination of Prison Misconduct Rates among Life-without-

Parole and Other Long-Term High-Security Inmates." *Criminal Justice and Behavior* 33 (2006): 683–705.

Darley, John. "Citizens' Assignments of Punishments for Moral Transgressions: A Case Study in the Psychology of Punishment." *Ohio State Journal of Criminal Law* 8 (2010): 101–117.

Dawes, John. "Dying with Dignity: Prisoners and Terminal Illness." *Illness, Crisis, & Loss* 10 (2002): 188–203.

Douglas, Mary. *Purity and Danger: An Analysis of Concepts of Pollution and Taboo.* London: Routledge, 2002.

Duff, R. Anthony. *Punishment, Communication, and Community.* Oxford: Oxford University Press, 2003.

Durkheim, Émile. *The Division of Labor in Society.* New York: Macmillan, 1984.

Erickson, Kai. *Wayward Puritans: A Study in the Sociology of Deviance.* Boston: Allyn & Bacon, 2004.

Evans, Tony, and Patti Wallace. "A Prison within a Prison? The Masculinity Narratives of Male Prisoners." *Men and Masculinities* 10 (2008): 484–507.

Ezell, Michael, and Lawrence Cohen. *Desisting from Crime.* Oxford: Oxford University Press, 2005.

Fazel, Seena, Tony Hope, Ian O'Donnell, Mary Piper, and Robin Jacoby. "Health of Elderly Male Prisoners: Worse Than the General Population, Worse Than Younger Prisoners." *Age and Ageing* 30 (2001): 403–407.

Fazel, Seena, John McMillan, and Ian O'Donnell. "Dementia in Prison: Ethical and Legal Implications." *Journal of Medical Ethics* 28 (2002): 156–159.

Ferguson, Robert. *Inferno: An Anatomy of American Punishment.* Cambridge, MA: Harvard University Press, 2014.

Flanagan, Timothy. "Dealing with Long-Term Confinement: Adaptive Strategies and Perspectives among Long-Term Prisoners." *Criminal Justice and Behavior* 8 (1981): 201–222.

Fleury-Steiner, Benjamin. *Dying Inside: The HIV/AIDS Ward at Limestone Prison.* Ann Arbor: University of Michigan Press, 2008.

Fleury-Steiner, Benjamin, and Jamie Longazel. *The Pains of Mass Imprisonment.* New York: Routledge, 2013.

Frase, Richard. "Punishment Purposes." *Stanford Law Review* 58 (2005:) 67–83.

Gallagher, Elaine. "Elders in Prison: Health and Well-Being of Older Inmates." *International Journal of Law and Psychiatry* 24 (2001): 325–333.

Garabino, James. *Listening to Killers: Lessons Learned from My Twenty Years as a Psychological Expert Witness in Murder Cases.* Oakland: University of California Press, 2015.

Garfinkel, Harold. "Conditions of Successful Degradation Ceremonies." *American Journal of Sociology* 61 (1956): 420–424.

Garland, David. *Punishment and Modern Society: A Study in Social Theory.* Chicago: University of Chicago Press, 1990.

Garvey, Stephen. "Punishment as Atonement." *UCLA Law Review* 46 (1999): 1801–1858.

George, Erin. *A Woman Doing Life: Notes from a Prison for Women.* Oxford: Oxford University Press, 2010.

Gey, Steven. "Justice Scalia's Death Penalty." *Florida State University Law Review* 20 (1992): 67–132.

Ghandnoosh, Nazgol. *Delaying a Second Chance: The Declining Prospects for Parole on Life Sentences.* Washington, DC: Sentencing Project, 2017.

Giordano, Peggy, Stephen Cernkovich, and Jennifer Rudolph. "Gender, Crime, and Desistance: Toward a Theory of Cognitive Transformation." *American Journal of Sociology* 107 (2002): 990–1064.

Goldberg, Elkhonon. *The Executive Brain: Frontal Lobes and the Civilized Mind.* Oxford: Oxford University Press, 2001.

Gottschalk, Marie. *Caught: The Prison State and the Lockdown of American Politics.* Princeton, NJ: Princeton University Press, 2015.

———. "Sentenced to Life: Penal Reform and the Most Severe Sanctions." *Annual Review of Law and Social Science* 9 (2013): 353–382.

Halleck, Seymour, and Ann Witte. "Is Rehabilitation Dead?" *Crime & Delinquency* 2 (1977): 372–383.

Hampton, Jean. "Correcting Harms versus Righting Wrongs: The Goal of Retribution." *UCLA Law Review* 39 (1992): 1659–1702.

———. "An Expressive Theory of Retribution." In *Retributivism and Its Critics*, edited by Wesley Craig, 1–25. Stuttgart, Ger.: Franz Steiner Verlag, 1992.

Haney, Craig. "The Psychological Impact of Incarceration: Implications for Postprison Adjustment." In *Prisoners Once Removed: The Impact of Incarceration on Children, Families and Communities*, edited by Jeremy Travis and Michelle Waul, 33–66. Washington, DC: Urban Institute, 2003.

———. *Reforming Punishment: Psychological Limits to the Pains of Imprisonment.* Washington, DC: American Psychological Association, 2009.

Harris, Alexes, Heather Evans, and Katherine Beckett. "Drawing Blood from Stones: Legal Debt and Social Inequality in the Contemporary United States." *American Journal of Sociology* 115 (2010): 1753–1799.

Harris, Alexes, Beth Huebner, Karin Martin, Mary Pattillo, Becky Pettit, Sarah Shannon, Bryan Sykes, Chris Uggen, and April Fernandes. *Monetary Sanctions in the Criminal Justice System*. Houston: John and Laura Arnold Foundation, 2017.

Harrison, Mary. "True Grit: An Innovative Program for Elderly Inmates." *Corrections Today* 68 (2006): 46–49.

Harrison, Mary, and Jim Benedetti. "Comprehensive Geriatric Programs in a Time of Shrinking Resources: 'True Grit' Revisited." *Corrections Today* 71 (2009): 44–47.

Harvard Law Review Association. "A Matter of Life and Death: The Effect of Life-without-Parole Statutes on Capital Punishment." *Harvard Law Review* 119 (2006): 1838–1854.

Hassine, Victor. *Life without Parole: Living and Dying in Prison Today*. Oxford: Oxford University Press, 2010.

Henry, Jessica. "Reducing Severe Sentences: The Role of Prison Programming in Sentencing Reform." *Criminology and Public Policy* 14 (2015): 397–405.

Herbert, Steve. "Inside or Outside? Expanding the Narratives about Life-Sentenced Prisoners." *Punishment and Society*, https://doi.org/10.1177/1462474517737048.

Hoffman, Heath, and George Dickinson. "Characteristics of Prison Hospice Programs in the United States." *American Journal of Hospice and Palliative Medicine* 28 (2011): 245–252.

Hulley, Susan, Ben Crewe, and Serena Wright. "Re-examining the Problems of Long-Term Imprisonment." *British Journal of Criminology* 56 (2016): 769–792.

Human Rights Watch. *Old behind Bars: The Aging Prison Population in the United States*. New York: Human Rights Watch, 2012.

Irwin, John. *Lifers: Seeking Redemption in Prison*. New York: Routledge, 2009.

————. *The Warehouse Prison: Disposal of the New Dangerous Class*. Los Angeles: Roxbury, 2005.

Jewkes, Yvonne. "Loss, Liminality and the Life Sentence: Managing Identify through a Disrupted Lifecourse." In *The Effects of Imprisonment*, edited by Alison Liebling and Shadd Maruna, 366–388. Portland, OR: Willan, 2005.

Johnson, Robert. *Hard Time: Understanding and Reforming the Prison*. Belmont, CA: Wadsworth, 2002.

Johnson, Robert, and Ania Dobrzanska. "Mature Coping among Life-Sentenced Inmates: An Exploratory Study of Adjustment Dynamics." *Corrections Compendium* 30 (2005): 8–13.

Johnson, Sara, Robert Blum, and Jay Giedd. "Adolescent Maturity and the Brain: The Promise and Pitfalls of Neuroscience Research in Adolescent Health Policy." *Journal of Adolescent Health* 45 (2009): 216–221.

Kaplan, Paul. *Murder Stories: Ideological Narratives in Capital Punishment*. Lanham, MD: Lexington Books, 2012.

Kauffman, Kelsey. *Prison Officers and Their World*. Cambridge MA: Harvard University Press, 1988.

Kazemian, Lila. "Desistance from Crime: Theoretical, Empirical, Methodological and Policy Considerations." *Journal of Contemporary Criminal Justice* 23 (2007): 5–27.

Kazemian, Lila, and Jeremy Travis. "Imperative for Inclusion of Long Termers and Lifers in Research and Policy." *Criminology and Public Policy* 14 (2015): 355–395.

Kerbs, John, and Jennifer Jolley. "A Commentary on Age Segregation for Older Prisoners: Philosophical and Pragmatic Considerations." *Criminal Justice Review* 34 (2009): 119–132.

Kleinig, John. *Punishment and Desert*. The Hague: Martinus Nijhoff, 1973.

Lamont, Julian. "The Concept of Desert in Distributive Justice." *Philosophical Quarterly* 44 (1994): 45–64.

Laub, John, and Robert Sampson. *Shared Beginnings, Divergent Lives: Delinquent Boys to Age 70*. Cambridge, MA: Harvard University Press, 2003.

———. "Understanding Desistance from Crime." *Crime and Justice* 28 (2001): 1–69.

LeBel, Thomas. "An Examination of the Impact of Formerly Incarcerated Persons Helping Others." *Journal of Offender Rehabilitation* 26 (2007): 1–24.

LeBel, Thomas, Ros Burnett, Shadd Maruna, and Shawn Bushway. "The 'Chicken and Egg' of Subjective and Social Factors in Desistance from Crime." *European Journal of Criminology* 5 (2008): 131–159.

LeBel, Thomas, Matt Richie, and Shadd Maruna. "Helping Others as a Response to Reconcile a Criminal Past: The Role of the Wounded

Healer in Prisoner Reentry Programs." *Criminal Justice and Behavior* 42 (2015): 108–120.

Leigey, Margaret. *The Forgotten Men: Serving a Life without Parole Sentence.* New Brunswick, NJ: Rutgers University Press, 2015.

Leigey, Margaret, and Michael Ryder. "The Pains of Permanent Imprisonment: Examining Perceptions of Confinement among Older Life without Parole Inmates." *International Journal of Offender Therapy and Comparative Criminology* 59 (2015): 726–742.

Lerman, Amy. *The Modern Prison Paradox: Politics, Punishment and Social Community.* Cambridge: Cambridge University Press, 2013.

Liebling, Alison. *Prisons and Their Moral Performance: A Study of Values, Quality, and Prison Life.* Oxford: Oxford University Press, 2004.

Liem, Marieke. *After Life Imprisonment: Reentry in the Era of Mass Incarceration.* New York: NYU Press, 2016.

———. "Homicide Offender Recidivism: A Review of the Literature." *Aggression and Violent Behavior* 18 (2013): 19–25.

Liem, Marieke, Margaret Zahn, and Lisa Tichavsky. "Criminal Recidivism among Homicide Offenders." *Journal of Interpersonal Violence* 29 (2014): 2630–2651.

Loeb, Susan, and Azzu AbuDagga. "Health-Related Research on Older Inmates: An Integrative Literature Review." *Research in Nursing and Health* 29 (2006): 556–565.

Loeb, Susan, Darrel Steffensmeier, and Cathy Kassab. "Predictors of Self-Efficacy and Self-Rated Health for Older Male Inmates." *Journal of Advanced Nursing* 67 (2011): 811–820.

Mackie, John. "Morality and the Retributive Emotions." *Criminal Justice Ethics* 1 (1982): 3–9.

Martinson, Robert. "What Works?—Questions and Answers about Prison Reform." *National Affairs* 1 (1974): 22–54.

Maruna, Shadd. *Making Good: How Ex-convicts Reform and Rebuild Their Lives.* Washington, DC: American Psychological Association, 2001.

Maruna, Shadd, and Heith Copes. "What Have We Learned from Five Decades of Neutralization Research?" *Crime and Justice* 32 (2005): 221–320.

Maruna, Shadd, Thomas LeBel, and Charles Lanier. "Generativity behind Bars: Some 'Redemptive Truth' about Prison Society. In *The Generative Society: Caring for Future Generations,* edited by Ed St. Aubin, Dan

McAdams, and Tae-Chang Kim, 131–151. Washington, DC: American Psychological Association, 2004.

Maschi, Tina, Sandy Gibson, Kristen Zgoba, and Keith Morgen. "Trauma and Life Event Stressors among Young and Older Adult Prisoners." *Journal of Correctional Health Care* 17 (2011): 160–172.

Maschi, Tina, Jung Kaw, Eunjeong Ko, and Mary Morrissey. "Forget Me Not: Dementia in Prison." *Gerontologist* 52 (2012): 441–451.

Maschi, Tina, Mary Beth Morrissey, Russ Immarigeon, and Samantha Sutfin. *Aging Prisoners: A Crisis in Need of Intervention.* New York: Fordham University Be the Evidence Project, 2013.

Mitchell, Barry, and Julian Roberts. *Exploring the Mandatory Life Sentence for Murder.* Oxford, U.K.: Hart, 2012.

Morris, Herbert. "Persons and Punishment." *The Monist* 52 (1968): 475–501.

National Research Council. *The Growth of Incarceration in the United States: Exploring Causes and Consequences.* Washington, DC: National Academies Press, 2014.

Nellis, Ashley. *The Color of Justice: Racial and Ethnic Disparity in Prisons.* Washington, DC: Sentencing Project, 2016.

———. *Life Goes On: The Historic Rise of Life Sentences in America.* Washington, DC: Sentencing Project, 2013.

———. *Still Life: America's Increasing Use of Life and Long-Term Sentences.* Washington, DC: Sentencing Project, 2017.

———. "Throwing away the Key: The Expansion of Life without Parole Sentences in the United States." *Federal Sentencing Reporter* 23 (2010): 27–32.

Nilsen, Eva. "Decency, Dignity and Desert: Restoring Ideals of Humane Punishment to Constitutional Discourse." *UC Davis Law Review* 41 (2007–2008): 111–165.

Nozick, Robert. *Philosophical Investigations.* Cambridge, MA: Harvard University Press, 1981.

Nussbaum, Martha. "Equity and Mercy." *Philosophy & Public Affairs* 22 (1993): 83–125.

Osborne Association. *The High Costs of Low Risk: The Crisis of America's Aging Prison Population.* New York: Osborne Association, 2014.

Page, Joshua. "Eliminating the Enemy: The Import of Denying Prisoners Access to Higher Education in Clinton's America." *Punishment & Society* 6 (2004): 357–378.

————. *The Toughest Beat: Politics, Punishment and the Prison Officers Union in California*. New York: Oxford University Press, 2011.

Palmer, Ted. *Correctional Intervention and Research: Current Issues and Future Prospects*. Lexington, MA: Lexington Books, 1978.

Paluch, James. *A Life for a Life*. Oxford: Oxford University Press, 2003.

Presser, Lois. "Violent Offenders, Moral Selves: Constructing Identities and Accounts in the Research Interview." *Social Problems* 51 (2004): 82–101.

Rasch, Wilfried. "The Effects of Indeterminate Detention: A Study of Men Sentenced to Life Imprisonment." *International Journal of Law and Psychiatry* 4 (1981): 417–431.

Rawls, John. "Two Concepts of Rules." *Philosophical Review* 64 (1955): 3–32.

Reimer, Glenda. "The Graying of the U.S. Prisoner Population." *Journal of Correctional Health Care* 14 (2008): 202–208.

Rikard, Robert, and Ed Rosenberg. "Aging Inmates: A Convergence of Trends in the American Criminal Justice System." *Journal of Correctional Health Care* 13 (2007): 150–162.

Ristroph, Alice. "Desert, Democracy and Sentencing Reform." *Journal of Criminal Law and Criminology* 96 (2006): 1293–1352.

Ruddell, Rick, Ian Broom, and Matthew Young. "Creating Hope for Life-Sentenced Prisoners." *Journal of Offender Rehabilitation* 49 (2010): 324–341.

Ryan, Meghan. "Proximate Retribution." *Houston Law Review* 48 (2012): 1049–1106.

Sapsford, Roger. *Life Sentence Prisoners: Reaction, Response and Change*. London: Open University Press, 1983.

Schinkel, Marguerite. *Being Imprisoned: Adaptation and Desistance*. London: Palgrave, 2014.

Schmid, Thomas, and Richard Jones. "Suspended Identity: Identity Transformation in a Maximum Security Prison." *Symbolic Interaction* 14 (1991): 415–432.

Serrill, Michael. "Is Rehabilitation Dead?" *Corrections Magazine* 1 (1975): 21–32.

Sexton, Lori. "Penal Subjectivities: Developing a Theoretical Framework for Penal Consciousness." *Punishment and Society* 17 (2015): 114–136.

Shafer-Landau, Russ. "Retributivism and Desert." *Pacific Philosophical Quarterly* 81 (2000): 189–214.

Shover, Neal. *Great Pretenders: Pursuits and Careers of Persistent Thieves*. Oxford, U.K.: Westview Press, 1996.

Simon, Jonathan. *Governing through Crime: How the War on Crime Transformed American Democracy and Created a Culture of Fear.* Oxford: Oxford University Press, 2009.

———. *Mass Incarceration on Trial.* New York: New Press, 2016.

Slattery, Brian. "The Myth of Retributive Justice." In *Retributivism and Its Critics,* edited by Wesley Craig, 27–34. Stuttgart, Ger.: Franz Steiner Verlag, 1992.

Smith, Philip. *Culture and Punishment.* Chicago: University of Chicago Press, 2008.

Sorenson, James, and Jonathan Marquart. "Future Dangerousness and Incapacitation." In *American's Experiment with Capital Punishment: Reflections on the Past, Present and Future of the Ultimate Penal Sanction,* edited by James Acker, Robert Bohm, and Charles Lanier, 283–300. Durham, NC: Carolina Academic Press, 2003.

Sorenson, James, and Robert Wrinkle. "No Hope for Parole: Disciplinary Infractions among Death-Sentenced and Life-without-Parole Inmates." *Criminal Justice and Behavior* 23 (1996): 542–552.

Sparks, Richard, Anthony Bottoms, and Will Hay. *Prisons and the Problem of Order.* Oxford, U.K.: Clarendon Press, 1996.

Steinberg, Laurence. "Should the Science of Adolescent Brain Development Inform Public Policy?" *American Psychologist* 64 (2009): 739–750.

Sykes, Gresham. *The Society of Captives: A Study of a Maximum Security Prison.* Princeton, NJ: Princeton University Press, 1958.

Toch, Hans. "Hypermasculinity and Prison Violence." In *Masculinities and Violence,* edited by Lee Bowker, 168–178. Thousand Oaks, CA: Sage, 1998.

———. "'I Am Not Now Who I Used to Be Then': Risk Assessment and the Maturation of Long-Term Prison Inmates." *Prison Journal* 90 (2010): 4–11.

———. *Living in Prison: The Ecology of Survival.* New York: Free Press, 1977.

Toch, Hans, and Kenneth Adams. *Acting Out: Maladaptive Behavior in Confinement.* Washington, DC: American Psychological Association, 2002.

Tonry, Michael. "Assessing the State of Mass Incarceration: Tipping Point or the New Normal?" *Criminology and Public Policy* 13 (2014): 567–577.

———. *Punishing Race.* Oxford: Oxford University Press, 2011.

Trammell, Rebecca. *Enforcing the Convict Code: Violence and Prison Culture.* Boulder, CO: Lynne Rienner, 2012.

Travis, Jeremy. "Assessing the State of Mass Incarceration: Tipping Point or the New Normal?" *Criminology and Public Policy* 13 (2014): 567–577.

Tyler, Tom. *Why People Obey the Law: Procedural Justice, Legitimacy and Compliance.* New Haven, CT: Yale University Press, 1990.

Tyler, Tom, and Yuen Huo. *Trust in the Law: Encouraging Public Cooperation with the Police and Courts.* New York: Russell Sage Foundation, 2002.

Vaughn, Barry. "The Internal Narrative of Desistance." *British Journal of Criminology* 47 (2007): 390–404.

Vaughn, Michael, and Linda Smith. "Practicing Penal Harm Medicine in the United States: Prisoners' Voices from Jail." *Justice Quarterly* 16 (1999): 175–231.

Walker, Nigel. *Why Punish?* Oxford: Oxford University Press, 1991.

Walker, Samuel, Cassia Spohn, and Miriam Delone. *The Color of Justice: Race, Ethnicity and Crime in America.* Boston: Cengage, 2011.

Watson, Roger, Anne Stimpson, and Tony Hostick, "Prison Health Care: A Review of the Literature." *International Journal of Nursing Studies* 41 (2004): 119–128.

White, William. "The History of Recovered People as Wounded Healers: The Era of Professionalization and Specialization." *Alcoholism Treatment Quarterly* 18 (2000): 1–25.

Williams, Brie, Karla Lindquist, Rebecca Sudore, Heidi Strupp, Donna Willmott, and Louise Walter. "Being Old and Doing Time: Functional Impairment and Adverse Experiences of Geriatric Female Prisoners." *Journal of the American Geriatrics Society* 54 (2006): 702–707.

Wilson, John, and Sharen Barboza. "The Looming Challenge of Dementia in Prisons." *Correct Care* 24 (2010): 10–13.

Wright, Kevin, and Laura Bronstein. "Creating Decent Prisons." *Journal of Offender Rehabilitation* 44 (2007): 1–16.

Yampolskaya, Svetlana, and Norma Winston. "Hospice Care in Prison: General Principles and Outcomes." *American Journal of Hospice and Palliative Medicine* 20 (2003): 290–296.

Zamble, Edward. "Behavior and Adaptation in Long-Term Prison Inmates: Descriptive Longitudinal Results." *Criminal Justice and Behavior* 12 (1992): 409–425.

Zimring, Franklin. *The Contradictions of American Capital Punishment.* Oxford: Oxford University Press, 2003.

Index

Made in the USA
Coppell, TX
25 September 2020